TOP50

EASY PIANO

praise & worship

Arranged by Carol Tornquist

Lanzen

Produced by
Alfred Music Publishing Co., Inc.
P.O. Box 10003
Van Nuys, CA 91410-0003
alfred.com

Printed in USA.

*No part of this book shall be reproduced, arranged, adapted, recorded, publicly performed, stored in a retrieval system,
or transmitted by any means without written permission from the publisher. In order to comply with copyright laws, please apply for
such written permission and/or license by contacting the publisher at alfred.com/permissions.*

ISBN-10: 0-7390-9129-8
ISBN-13: 978-0-7390-9129-6

Cover art: Grunge religious background © Shutterstock / Genotar

 Alfred Cares. Contents printed on 100% recycled paper.

TABLE OF CONTENTS

10,000 REASONS

(Bless the Lord)

Words and Music by
Matt Redman and Jonas Myrin
Arranged by Carol Tornquist

© 2011 SHOUT! PUBLISHING (APRA) (Administered in the U.S. and Canada at EMICMGPublishing.com),
THANKYOU MUSIC (PRS) (Administered worldwide at EMICMGPublishing.com excluding Europe which is Administered at kingswaysongs.com),
WORSHIPTOGETHER.COM SONGS, SIXSTEPS MUSIC and SAID AND DONE MUSIC (Administered at EMICMGPublishing.com)
All Rights Reserved   Used by Permission

6

Verse 3:
And on that day when my strength is failing,
The end draws near and my time has come;
Still, my soul will sing Your praise unending,
Ten thousand years and then forevermore.
(To Chorus:)

AMAZING GRACE
(My Chains Are Gone)

Words and Music by
Chris Tomlin and Louie Giglio
Arranged by Carol Tornquist

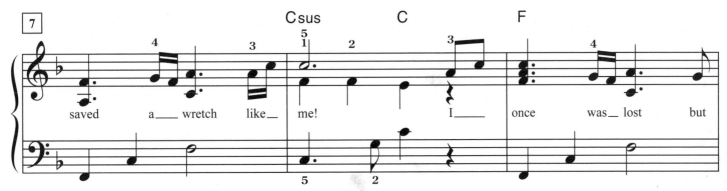

© 2006 WORSHIPTOGETHER.COM SONGS, SIXSTEPS MUSIC and VAMOS PUBLISHING
All Rights Administered at EMICMGPublishing.com
All Rights Reserved   Used by Permission

BE THE CENTRE

Words and Music by Michael Frye
Arranged by Carol Tornquist

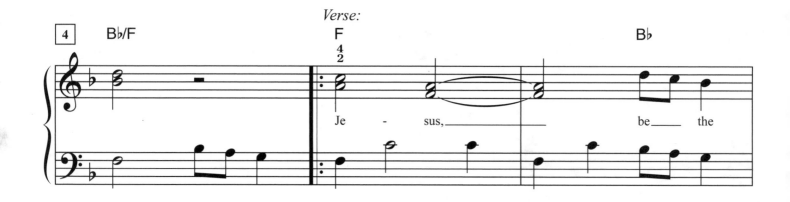

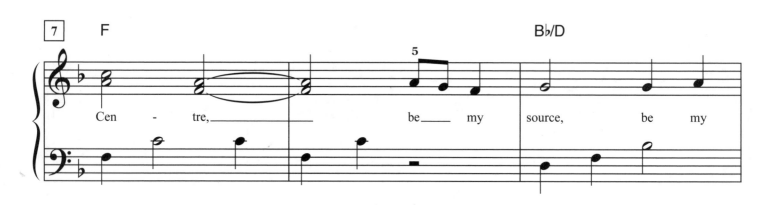

© 1999 VINEYARD SONGS (UK/EIRE) (PRS)
Administered in North America by MUSIC SERVICES, INC.
All Rights Reserved   Used by Permission

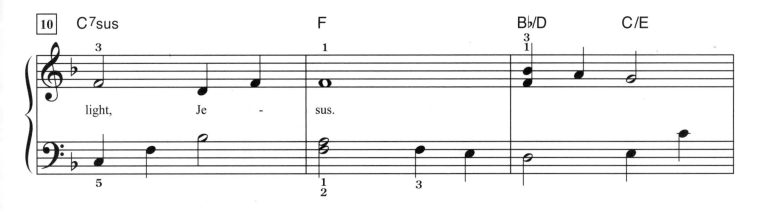

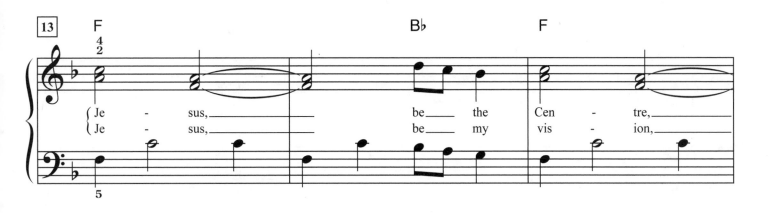

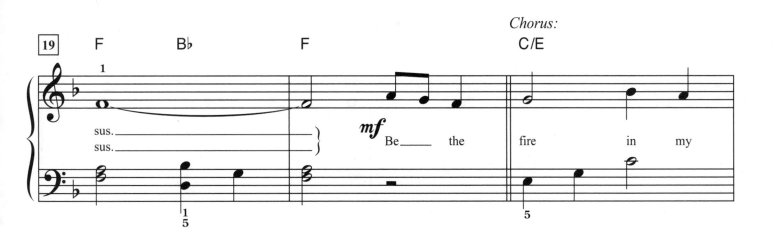

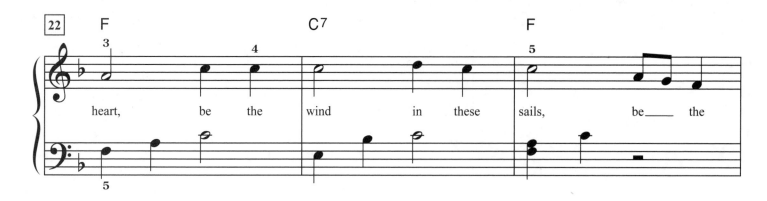

22 F · · C⁷ · · F ·

heart, be the wind in these sails, be____ the

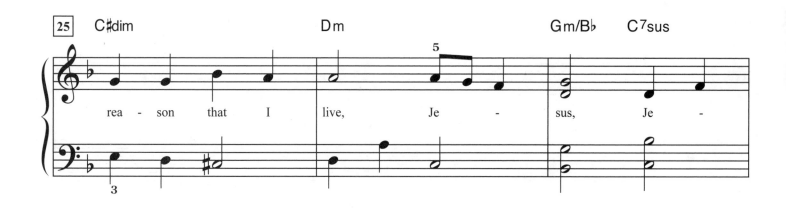

25 C♯dim · · Dm · · Gm/B♭ C⁷sus

rea - son that I live, Je - sus, Je -

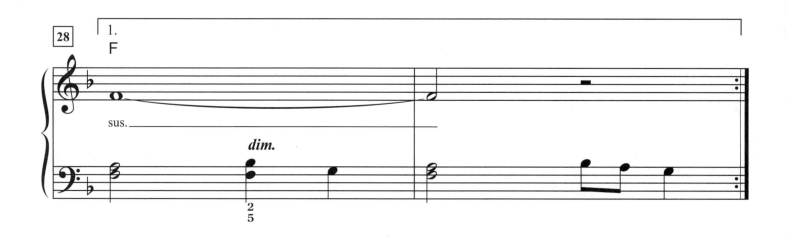

28 1.
F

sus._____
dim.

2
5

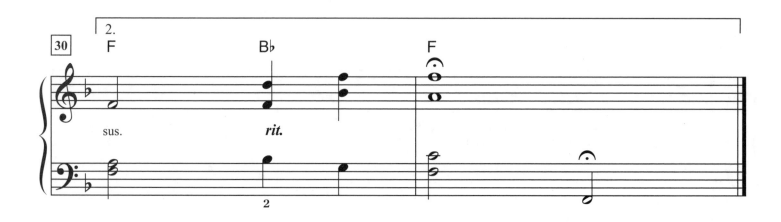

30 2.
F · · B♭ · · F ·

sus. *rit.*

2

BETTER IS ONE DAY

Words and Music by Matt Redman
Arranged by Carol Tornquist

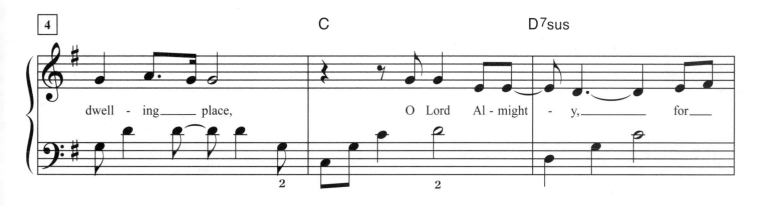

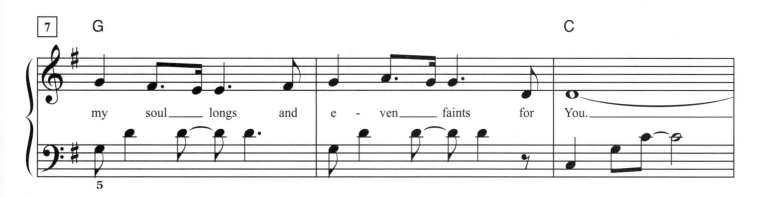

© 1995 THANKYOU MUSIC (PRS) (Administered worldwide at EMICMGPublishing.com excluding Europe which is administered by kingswaysongs.com) All Rights Reserved   Used by Permission

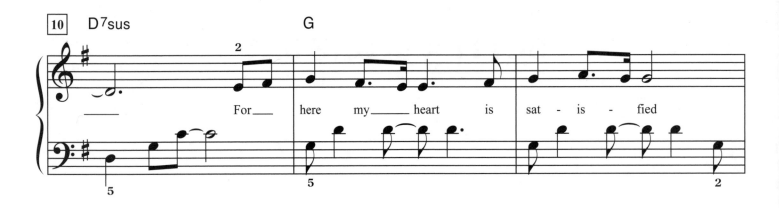

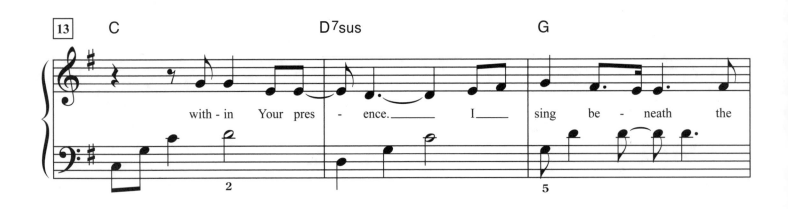

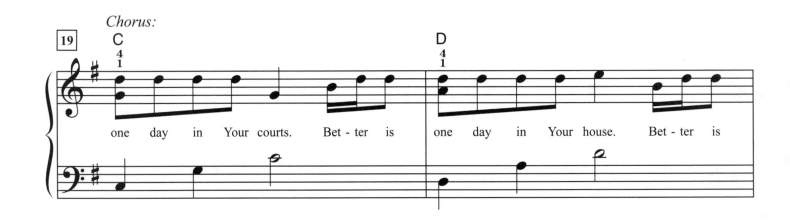

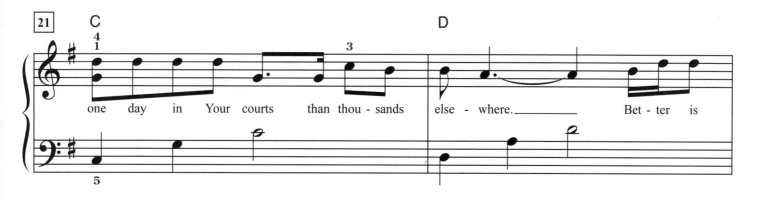

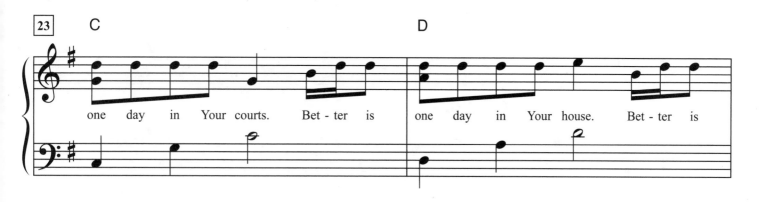

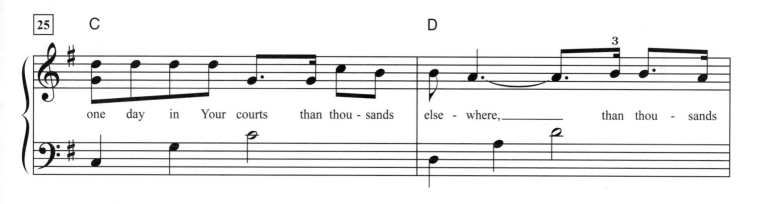

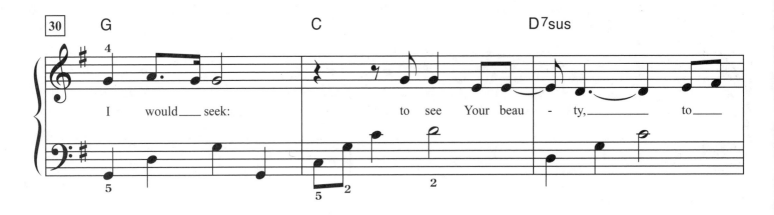

Chorus:

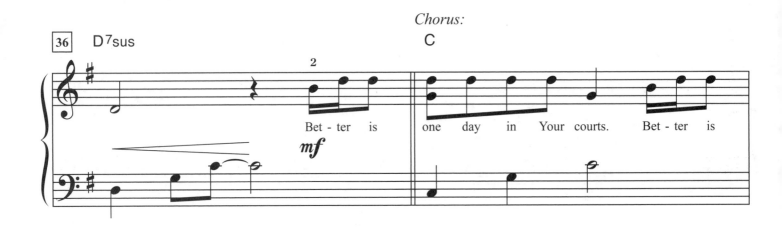

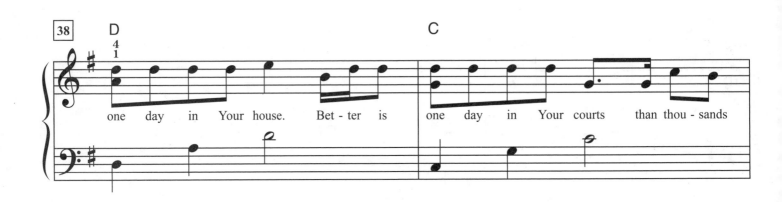

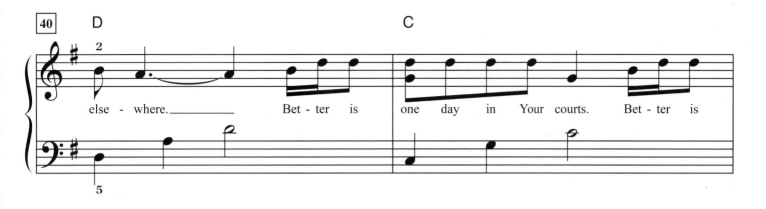

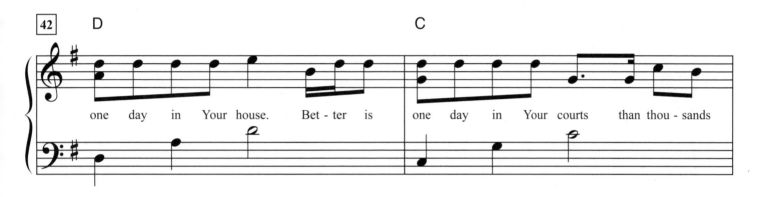

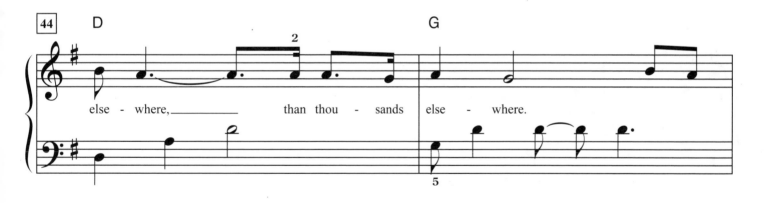

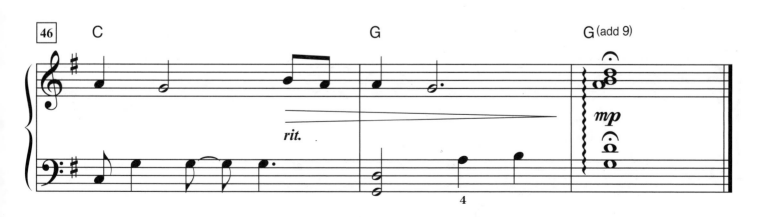

BEAUTIFUL ONE

Words and Music by Tim Hughes
Arranged by Carol Tornquist

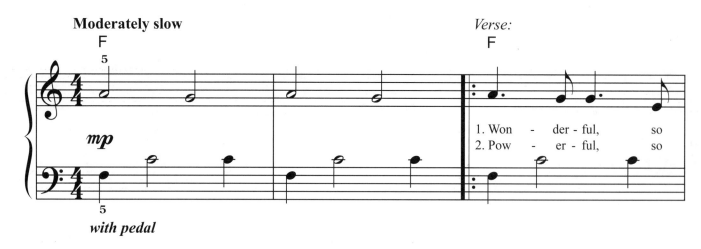

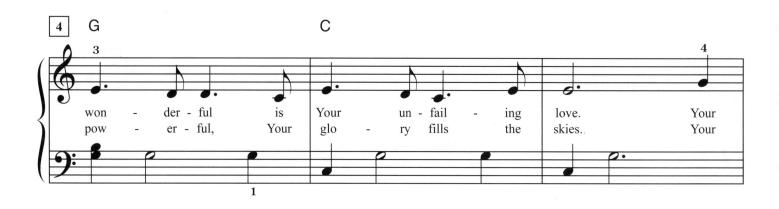

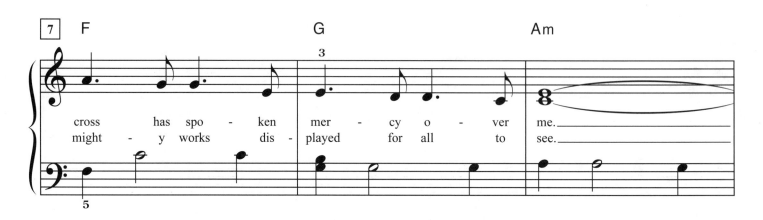

© 2002 THANKYOU MUSIC (PRS) (Administered worldwide at EMICMGPublishing.com
excluding Europe which is administered by kingswaysongs.com)
All Rights Reserved   Used by Permission

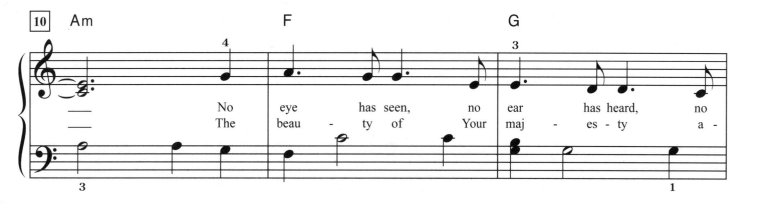

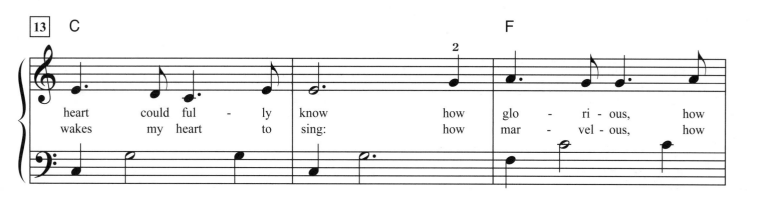

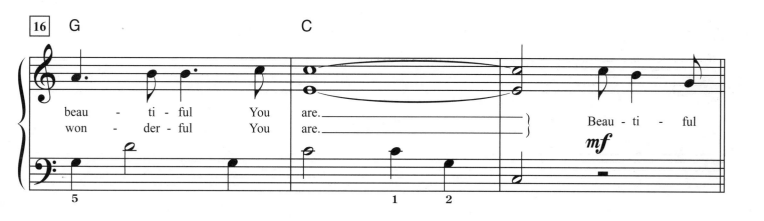

Chorus:

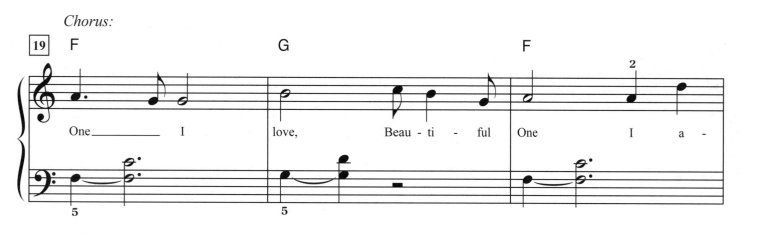

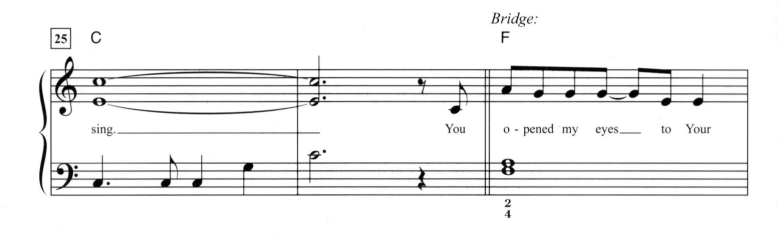

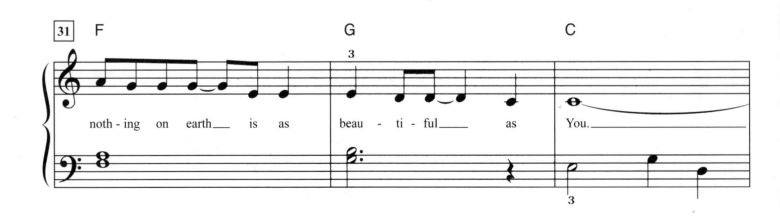

Chorus:

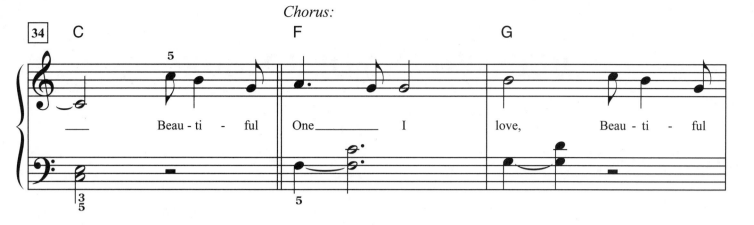

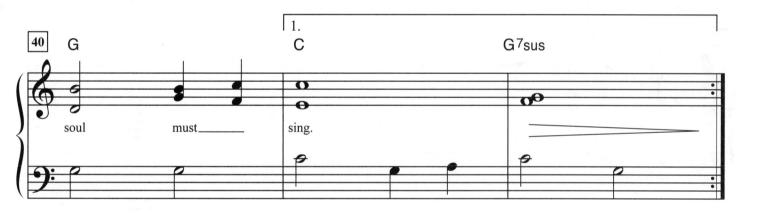

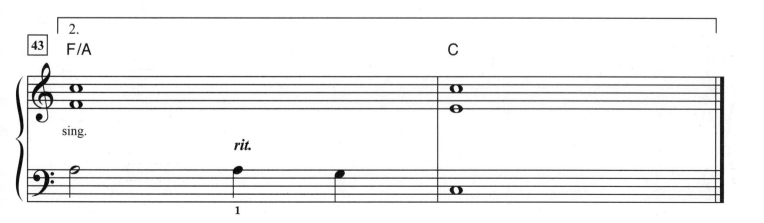

BLESSED BE YOUR NAME

Words and Music by
Beth Redman and Matt Redman
Arranged by Carol Tornquist

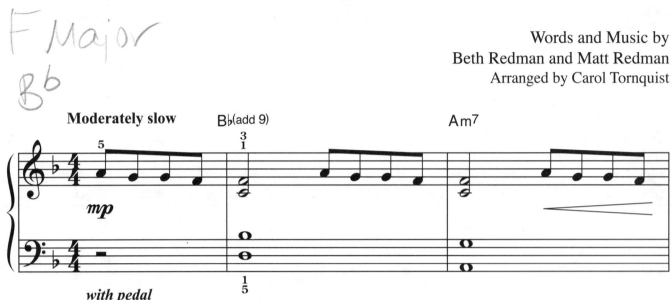

© 2002 THANKYOU MUSIC (PRS) (Administered worldwide at EMICMGPublishing.com
excluding Europe which is administered by kingswaysongs.com)
All Rights Reserved   Used by Permission

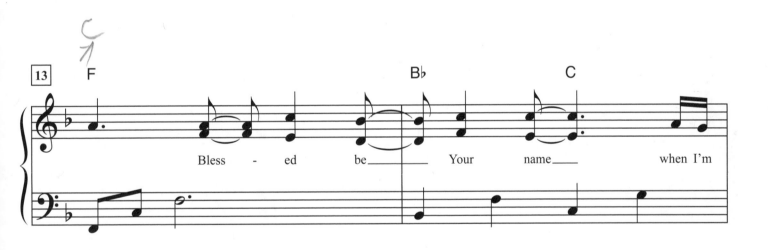

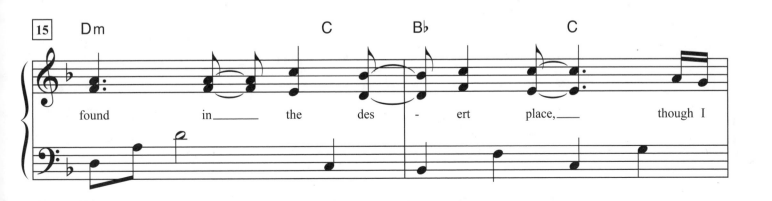

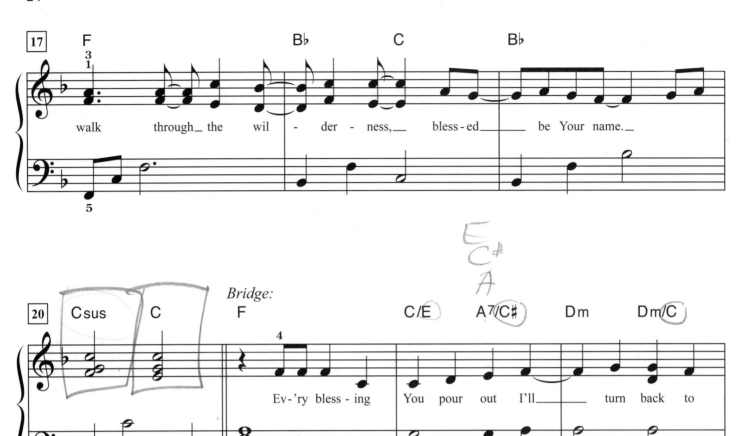

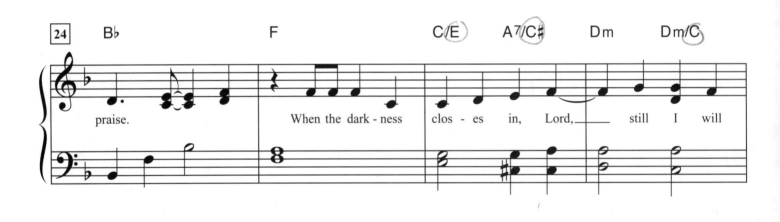

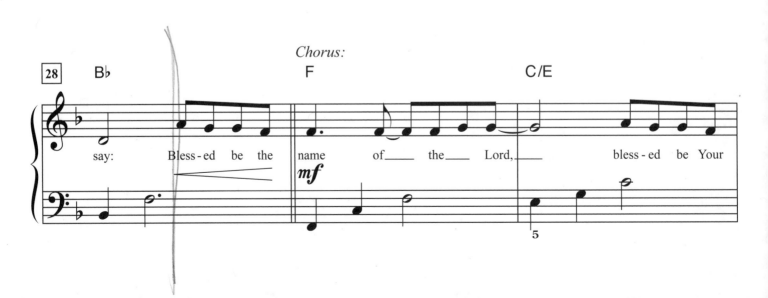

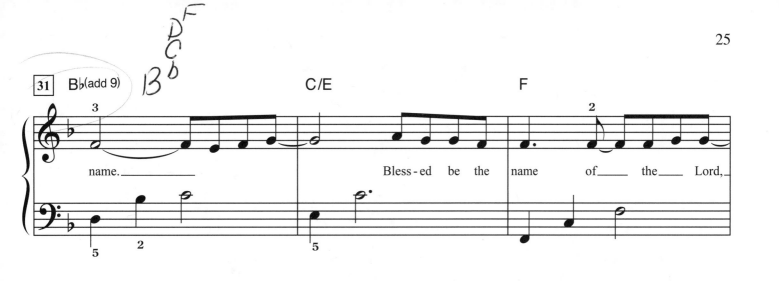

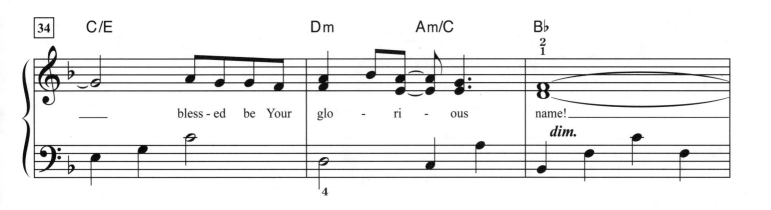

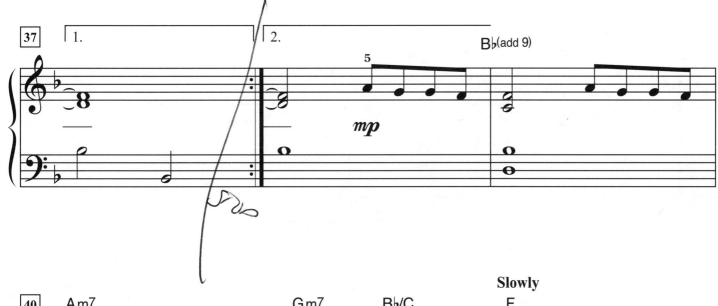

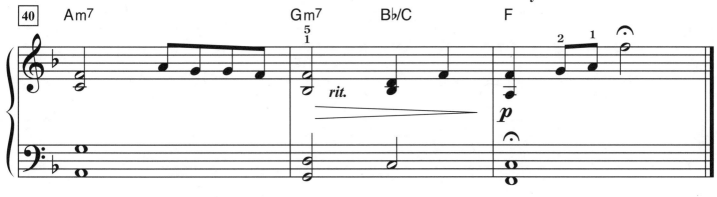

BLESSINGS

Words and Music by Laura Mixon Story
Arranged by Carol Tornquist

© 2011 NEW SPRING PUBLISHING (ASCAP) and LAURA STORIES (ASCAP)
All Rights Administered Worldwide by NEW SPRING PUBLISHING (ASCAP)
All Rights Reserved   Used by Permission

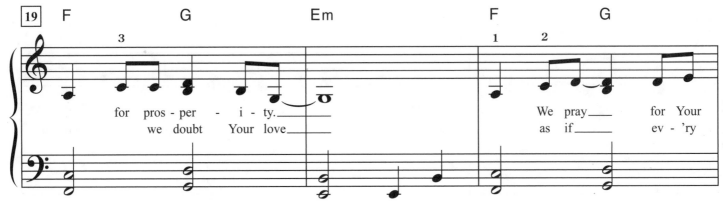

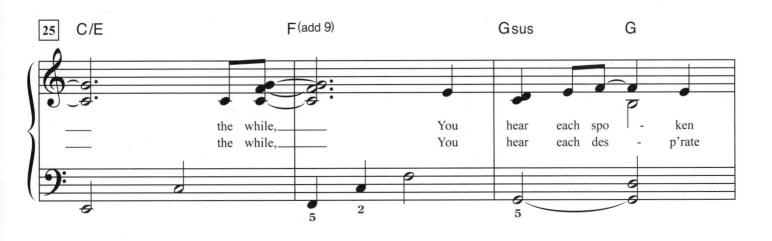

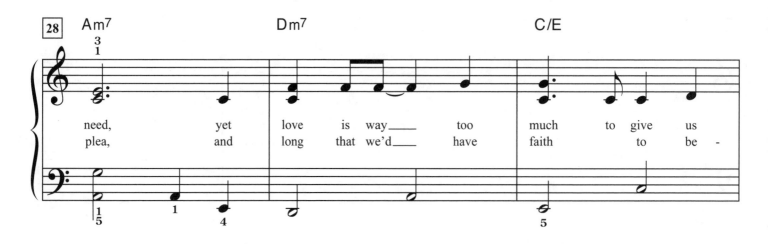

need,   yet   love   is   way____   too   much   to   give   us
plea,   and   long   that we'd____   have   faith   to   be -

Chorus:

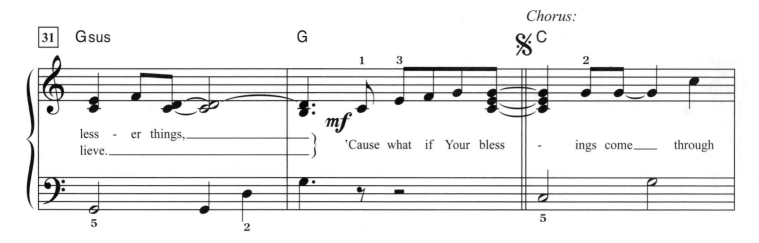

less - er   things,_____   'Cause what if Your bless - ings come____ through
lieve._____

mf

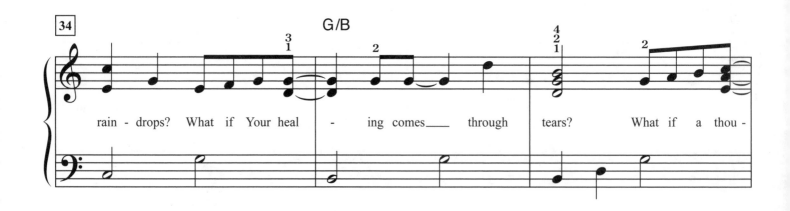

rain - drops? What if Your heal - ing comes____ through tears?   What if a thou-

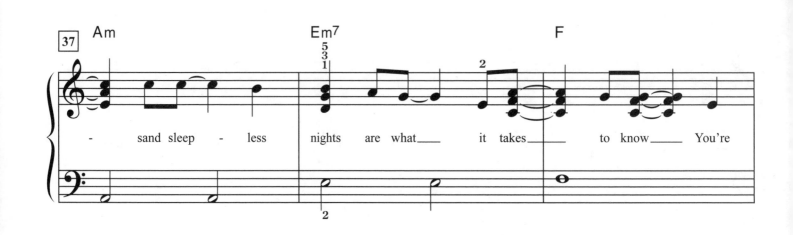

- sand sleep - less   nights   are what____   it takes_____   to know____   You're

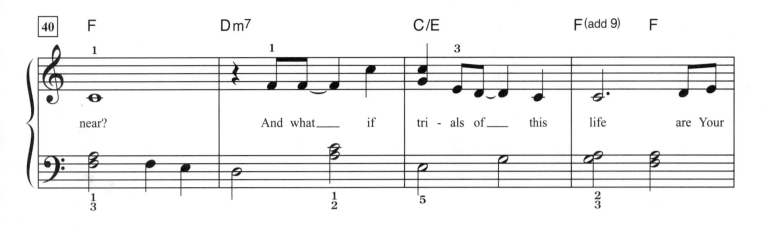

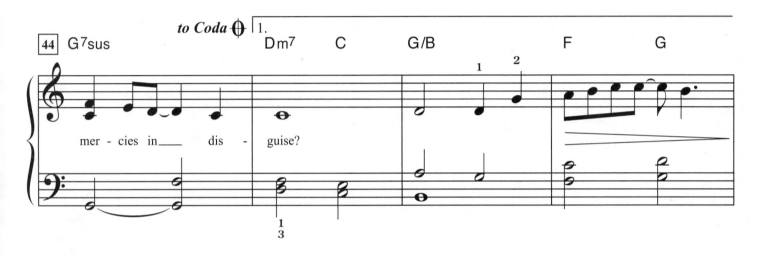

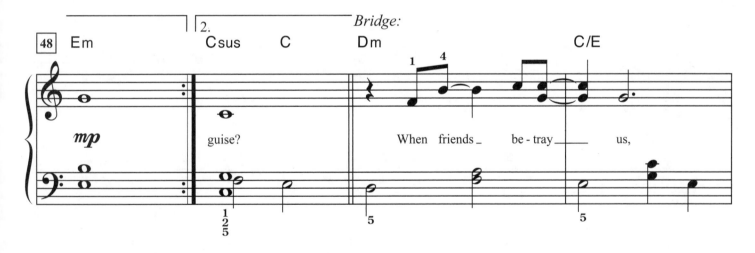

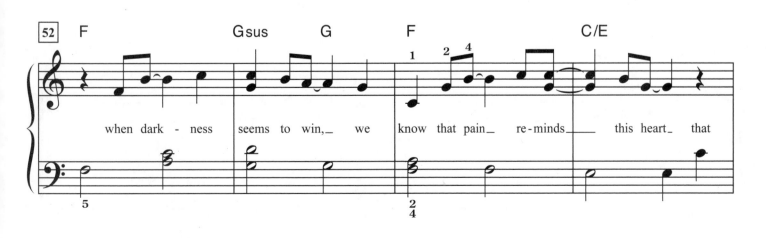

BREATHE

Words and Music by Marie Barnett
Arranged by Carol Tornquist

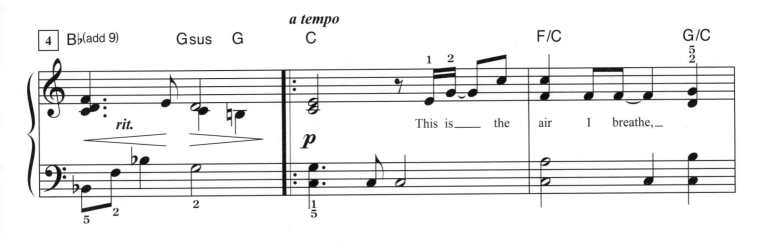

This is___ the air I breathe,___

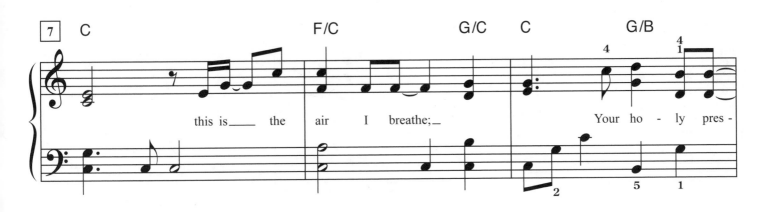

this is___ the air I breathe;___ Your ho-ly pres-

© 1995 MERCY/VINEYARD PUBLISHING
All Rights for North America Administered by MUSIC SERVICES, INC. on behalf of VINEYARD MUSIC USA
All Rights Reserved   Used by Permission

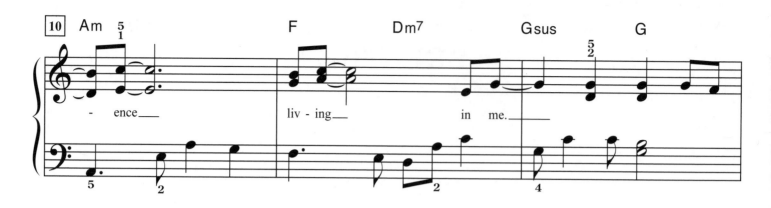

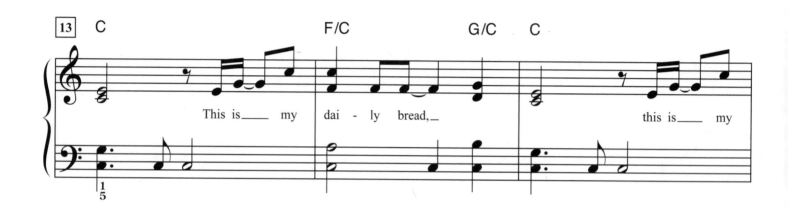

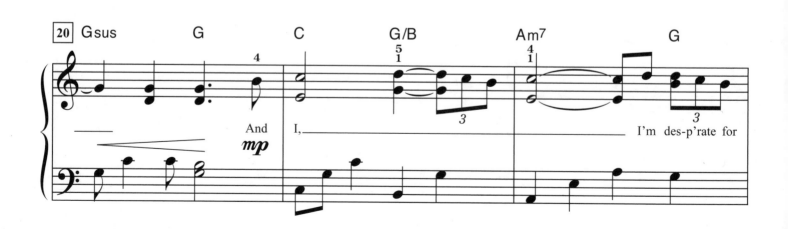

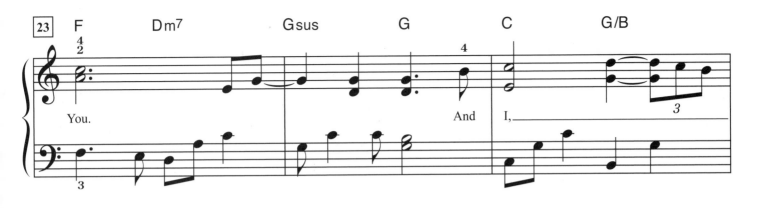

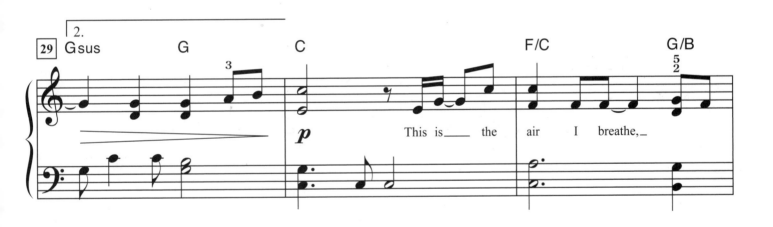

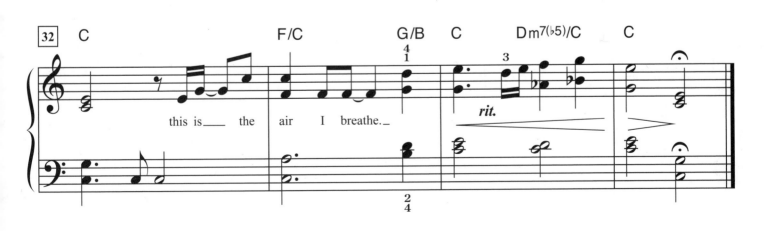

COME, NOW IS THE TIME TO WORSHIP

Words and Music by Brian Doerksen
Arranged by Carol Tornquist

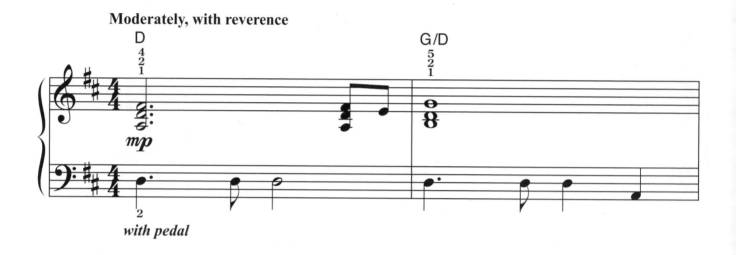

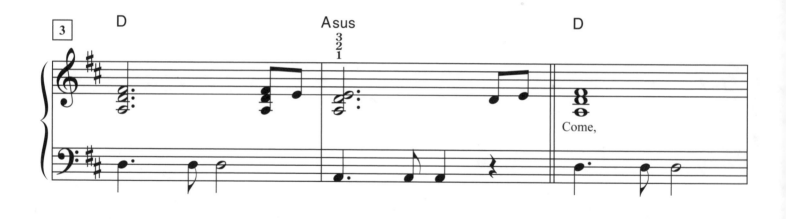

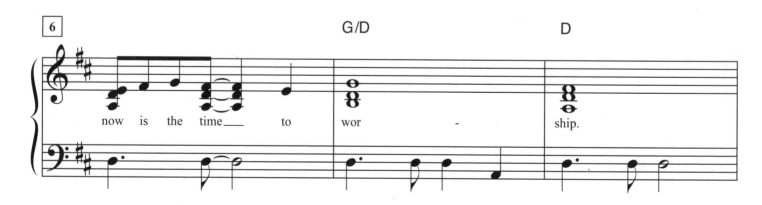

© 1998 VINEYARD SONGS (UK/EIRE) (PRS)
Administered in North America by MUSIC SERVICES, INC.
All Rights Reserved   Used by Permission

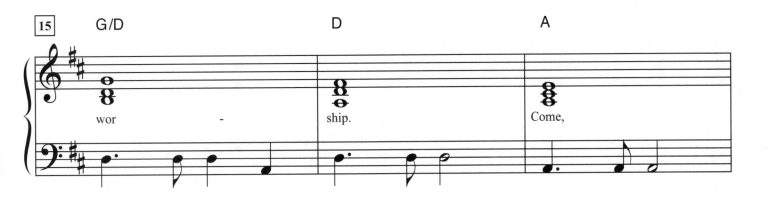

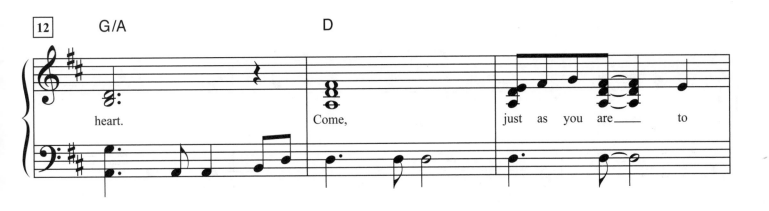

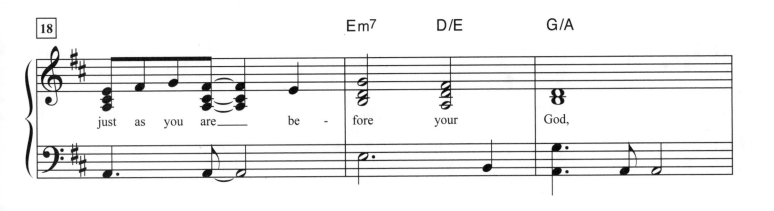

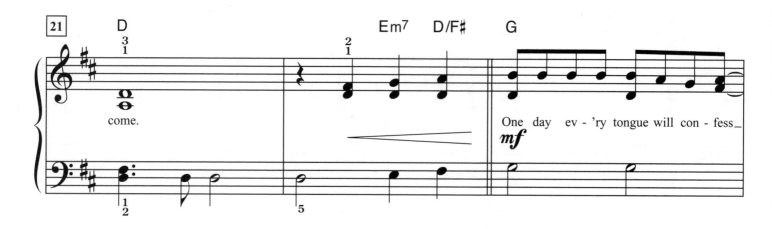

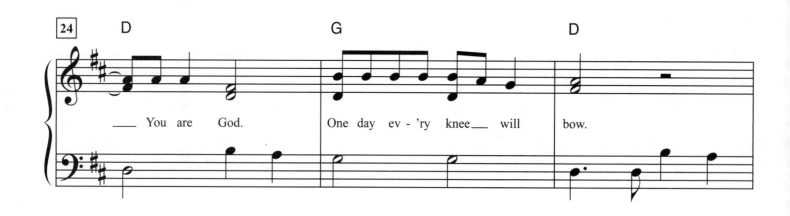

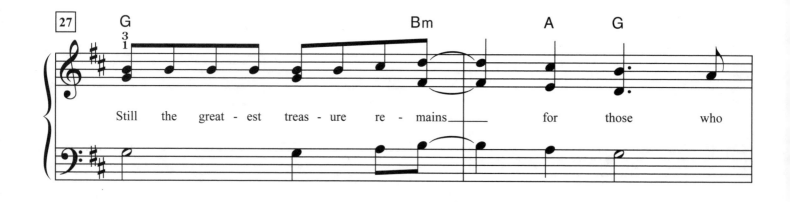

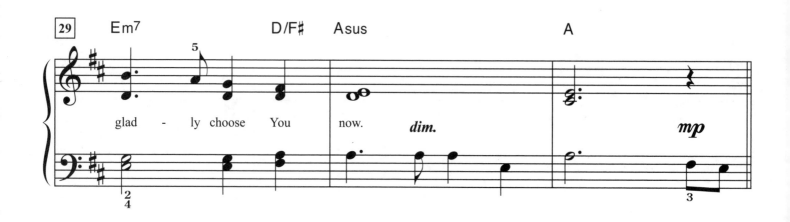

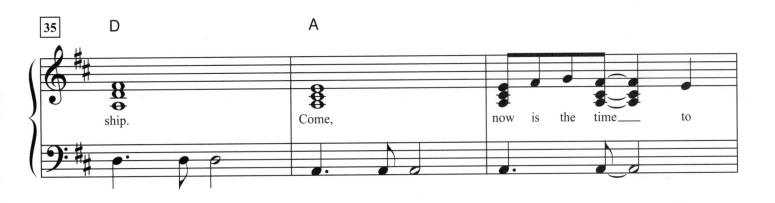

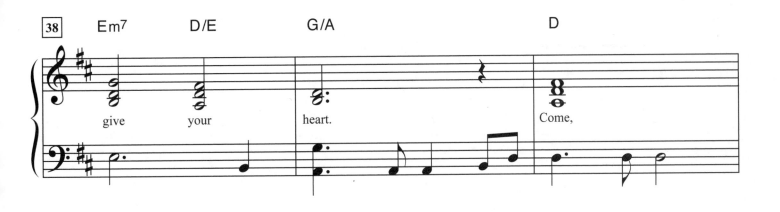

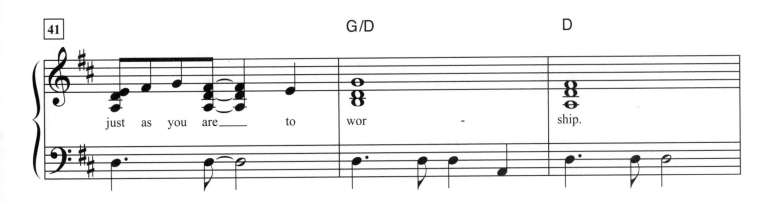

38

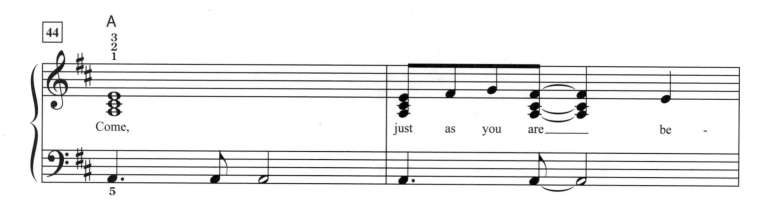

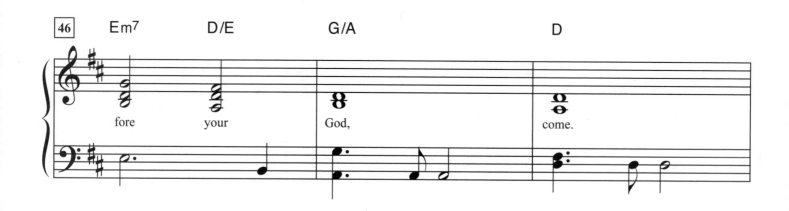

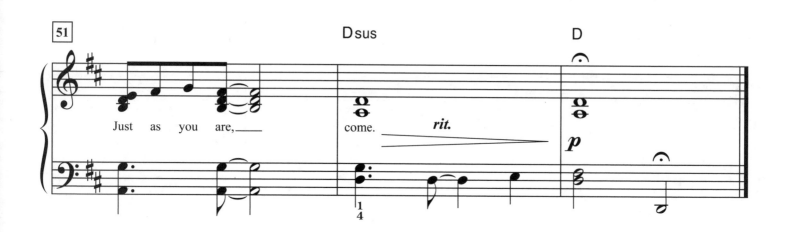

CRY OF MY HEART

Words and Music by Terry Butler
Arranged by Carol Tornquist

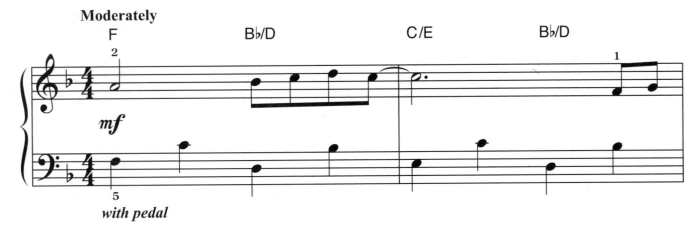

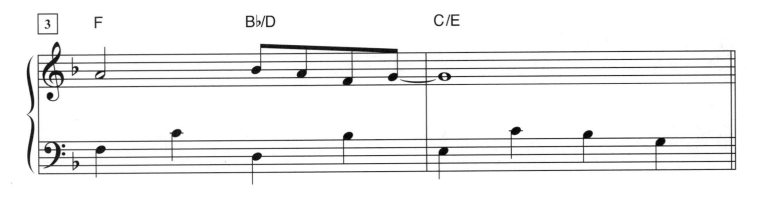

Chorus:

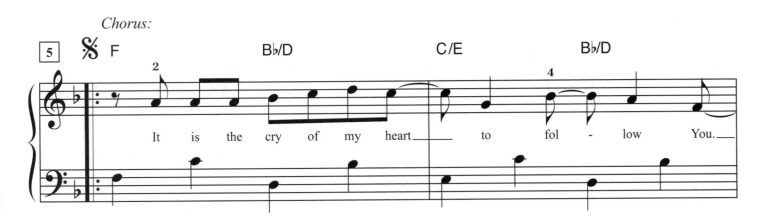

It is the cry of my heart___ to fol - low You.___

© 1991 MERCY/VINEYARD PUBLISHING
All Rights for North America Administered by MUSIC SERVICES, INC. on behalf of VINEYARD MUSIC USA
All Rights Reserved   Used by Permission

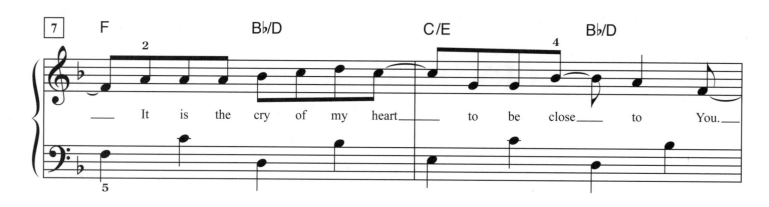

7 | F ... Bb/D ... C/E ... Bb/D

It is the cry of my heart___ to be close___ to You.___

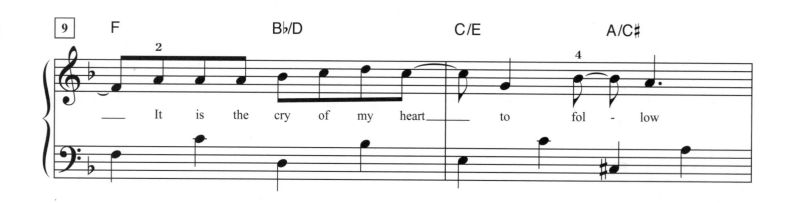

9 | F ... Bb/D ... C/E ... A/C#

It is the cry of my heart___ to fol - low

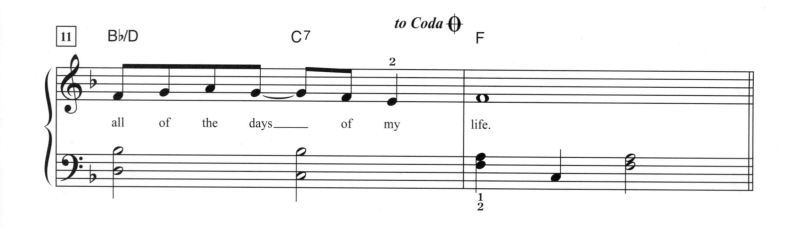

11 | Bb/D ... C7 ... *to Coda* ... F

all of the days___ of my life.

Verse:

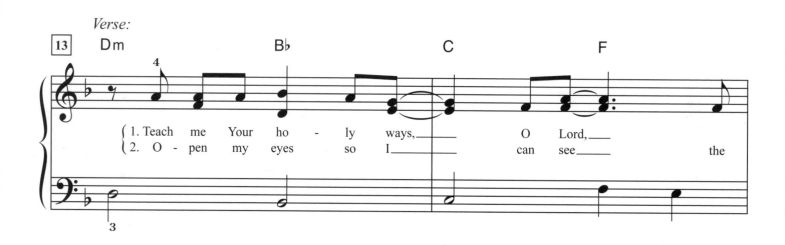

13 | Dm ... Bb ... C ... F

1. Teach me Your ho - ly ways,___ O Lord,___
2. O - pen my eyes so I___ can see___ the

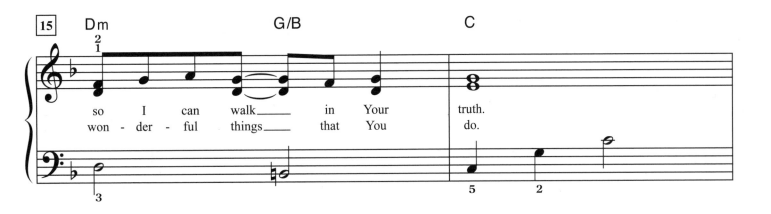

so I can walk____ in Your truth.
won - der - ful things____ that You do.

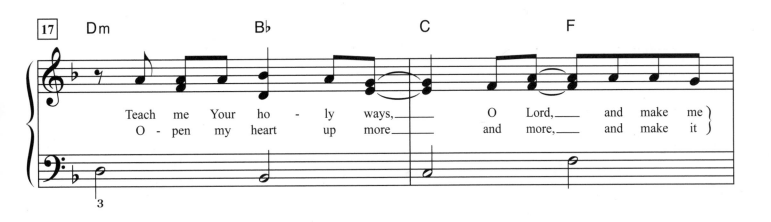

Teach me Your ho - ly ways,____ O Lord,____ and make me
O - pen my heart up more____ and more,____ and make it

D.S. al Coda

whol - ly de - vot - ed to You.   You.

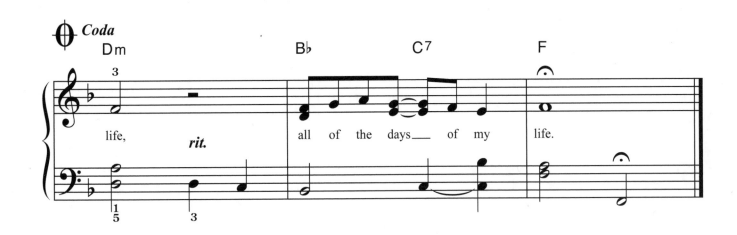

Coda

life,   *rit.*   all of the days____ of my   life.

DRAW ME CLOSE

Words and Music by Kelly Carpenter
Arranged by Carol Tornquist

© 1994 MERCY/VINEYARD PUBLISHING (ASCAP)
Administered in North America by MUSIC SERVICES, INC. on behalf of VINEYARD MUSIC USA
All Rights Reserved   Used by Permission

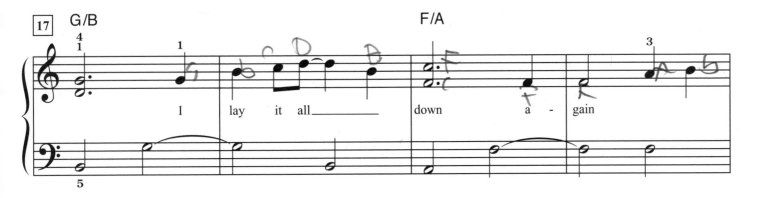

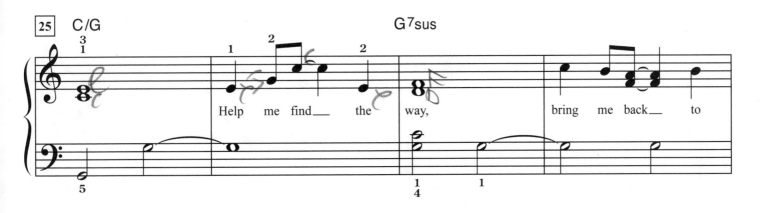

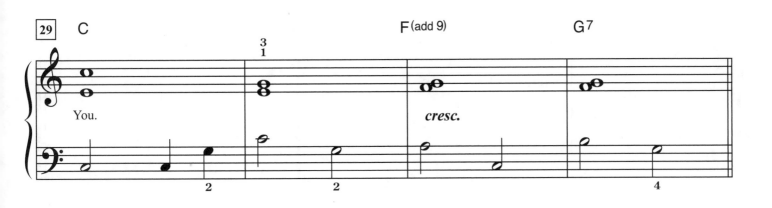

Chorus:

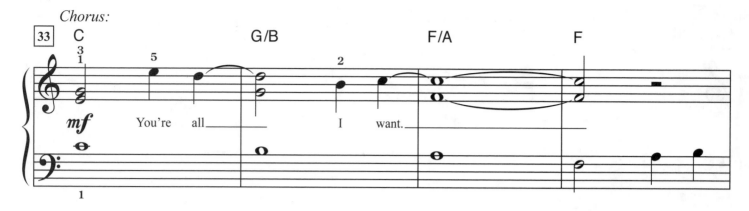

You're all__ I want.

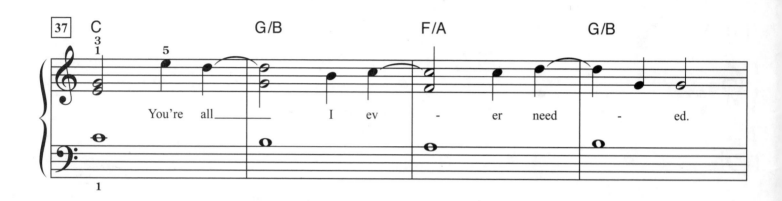

You're all__ I ev - er need - ed.

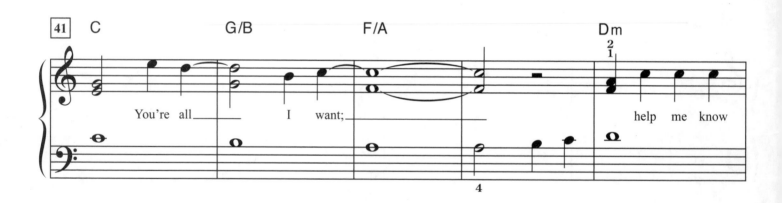

You're all__ I want; help me know

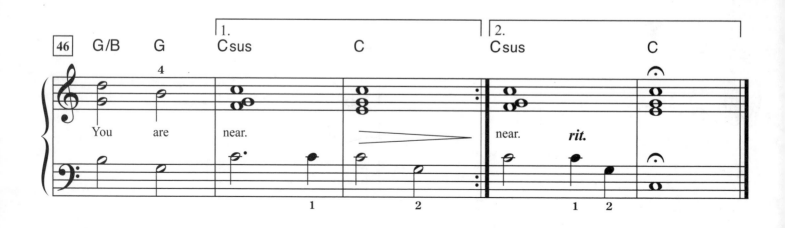

You are near. near. *rit.*

EVERLASTING GOD

Words and Music by
Brenton Brown and Ken Riley
Arranged by Carol Tornquist

© 2005 THANKYOU MUSIC (PRS) (Administered worldwide at EMICMGPublishing.com
excluding Europe which is administered by kingswaysongs.com)
All Rights Reserved   Used by Permission

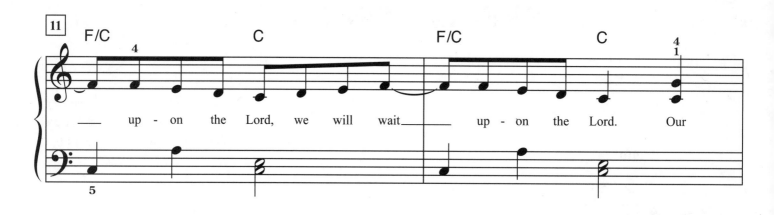

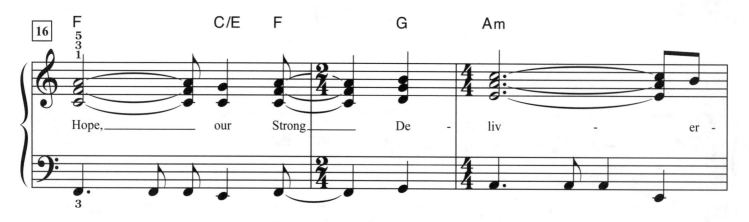

Chorus:

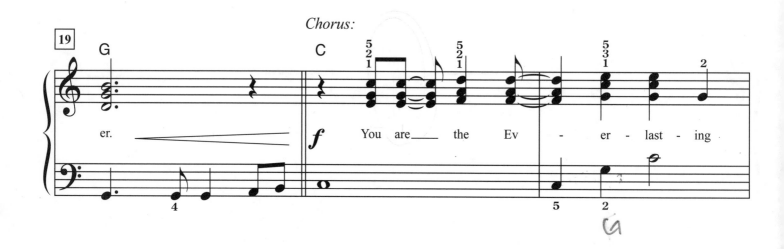

FOREVER

Words and Music by Chris Tomlin
Arranged by Carol Tornquist

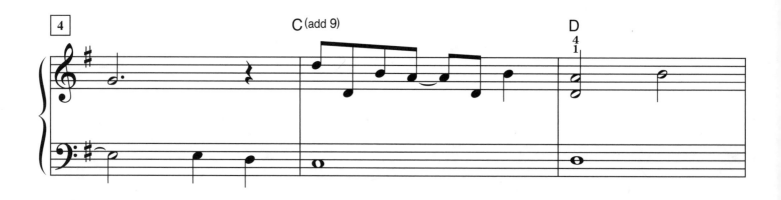

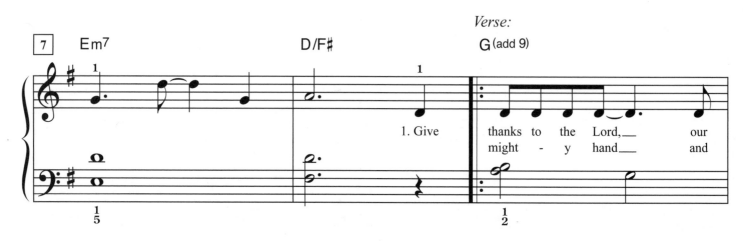

© 2001 WORSHIPTOGETHER.COM SONGS and SIXSTEPS MUSIC
All Rights Administered at EMICMGPublishing.com
All Rights Reserved   Used by Permission

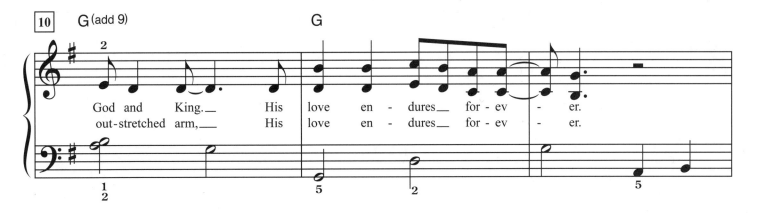

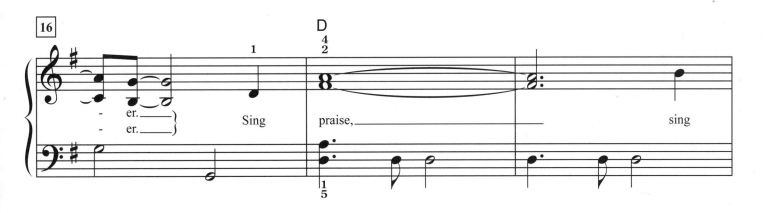

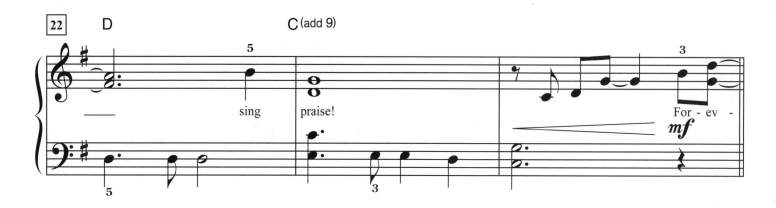

Chorus:

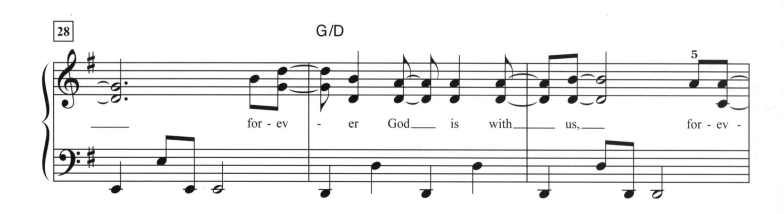

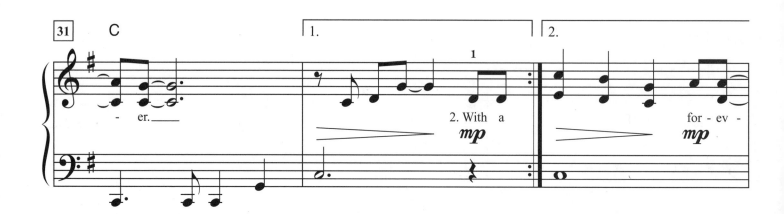

-er!____

for - ev - er!____

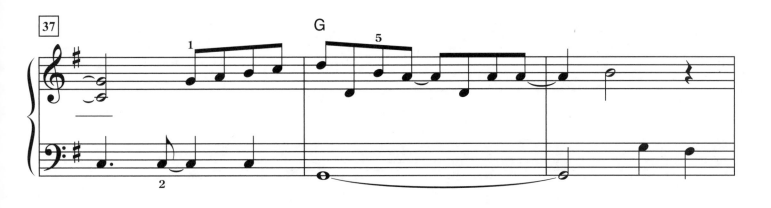

Em7

C (add 9)

dim.

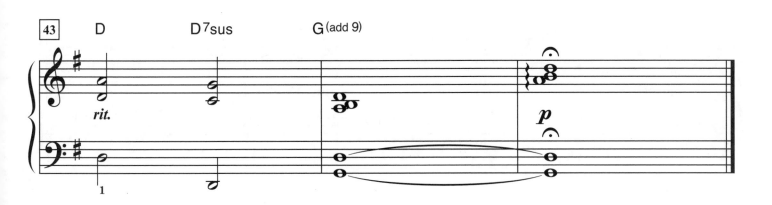

D   D7sus   G (add 9)

rit.   p

GIVE THANKS

Words and Music by Henry Smith
Arranged by Carol Tornquist

© 1978 INTEGRITY'S HOSANNA! MUSIC
All Rights Administered at EMICMGPublishing.com
All Rights Reserved   Used by Permission

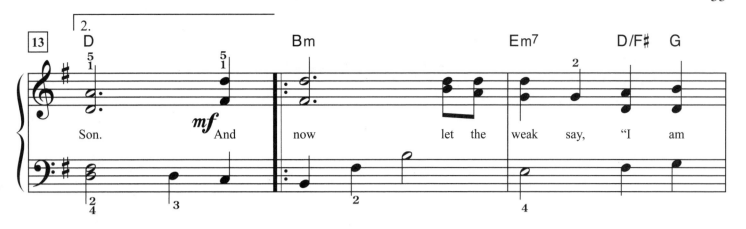

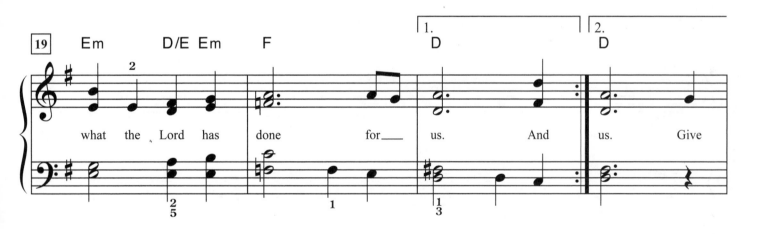

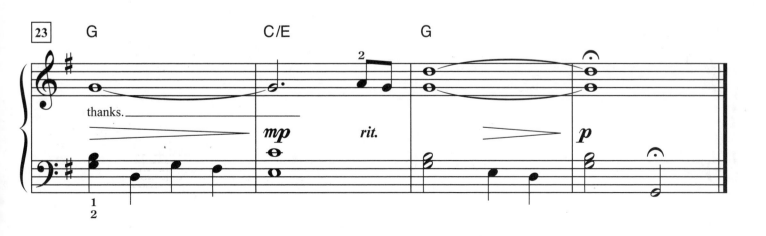

GOD OF WONDERS

Words and Music by
Marc Byrd and Steve Hindalong
Arranged by Carol Tornquist

Moderately slow
Verse:

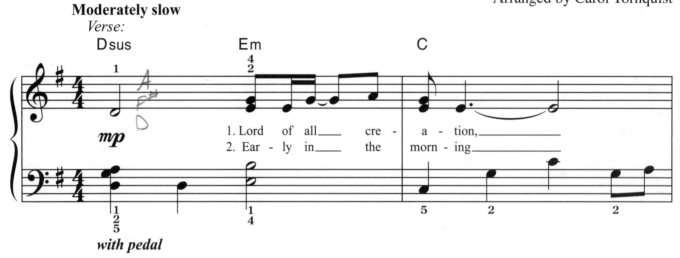

1. Lord of all___ cre - a - tion,_____
2. Ear - ly in___ the morn - ing_____

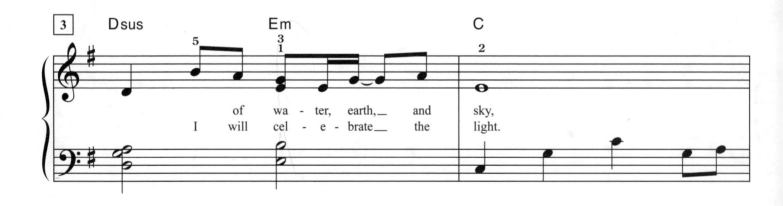

of wa - ter, earth,___ and sky,
I will cel - e - brate___ the light.

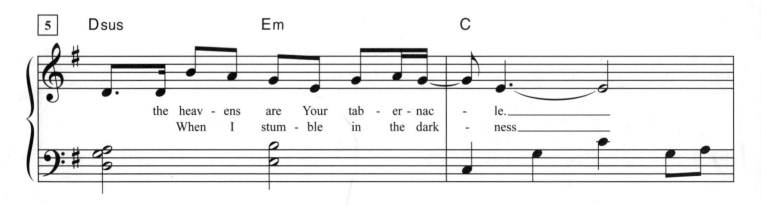

the heav - ens are Your tab - er - nac - le._____
When I stum - ble in the dark - ness_____

© 2000 STORM BOY MUSIC, MEAUX MERCY and NEW SPRING PUBLISHING
All Rights for STORM BOY MUSIC and MEAUX MERCY Administered at EMICMGPublishing.com
All Rights Reserved   Used by Permission

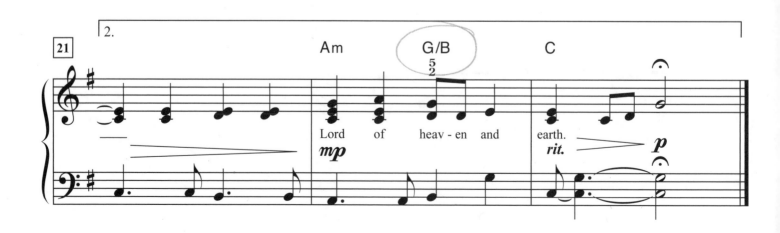

GREAT IS THE LORD

Words and Music by
Michael W. Smith and Deborah D. Smith
Arranged by Carol Tornquist

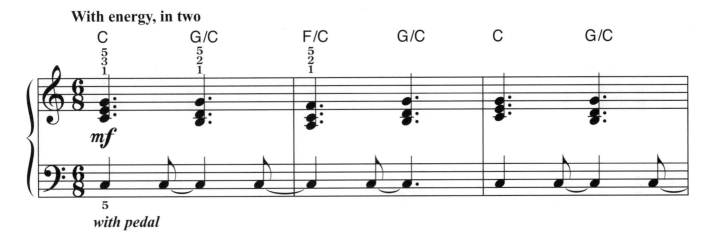

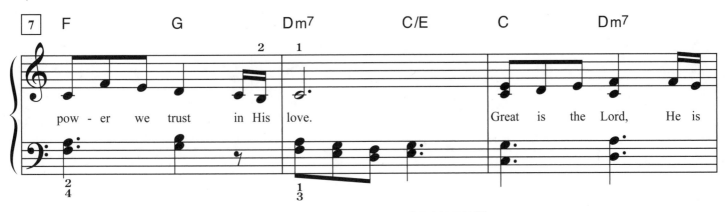

© 1982 MEADOWGREEN MUSIC COMPANY
All Rights Administered at EMICMGPublishing.com
All Rights Reserved   Used by Permission

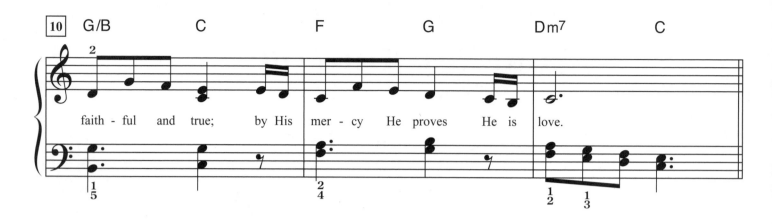

faith - ful and true; by His mer - cy He proves He is love.

Chorus:

Great is the Lord and wor - thy of glo - ry! Great is the Lord and

wor - thy of praise. Great is the Lord; now lift up your voice, now

cresc.

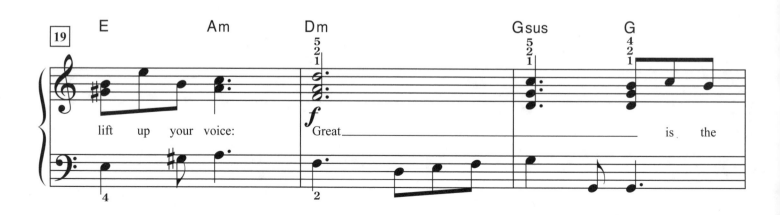

lift up your voice: *f* Great_____ is the

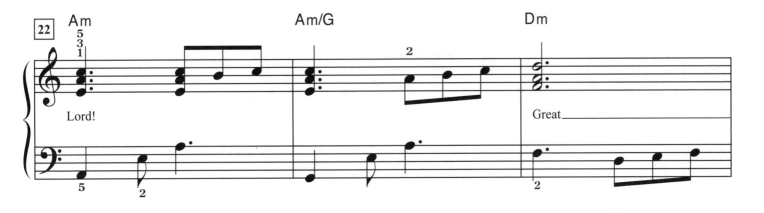

Lord! Great_____

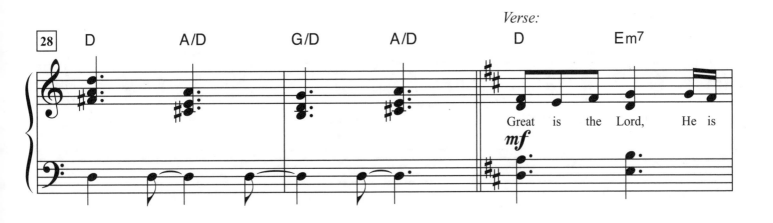

_____ is the Lord! *dim.*

Verse:

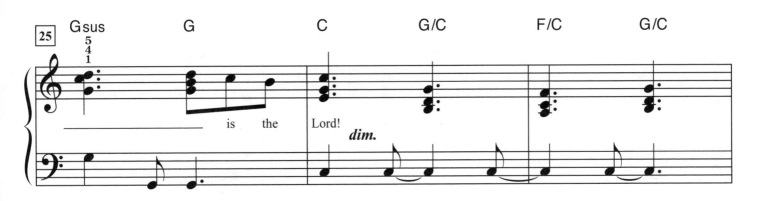

Great is the Lord, He is *mf*

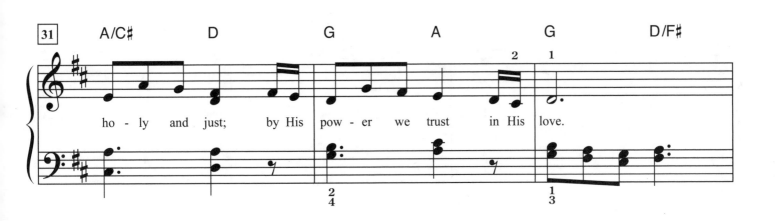

ho - ly and just; by His pow - er we trust in His love.

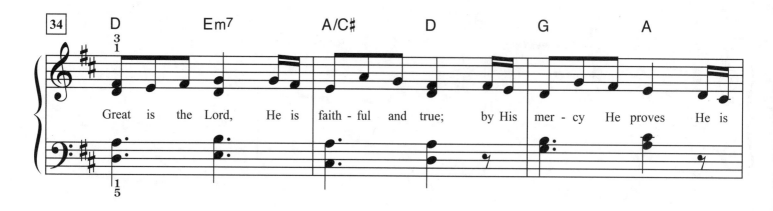

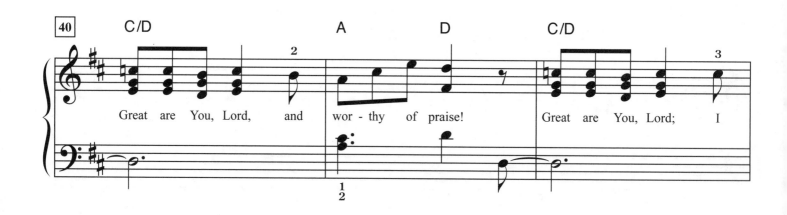

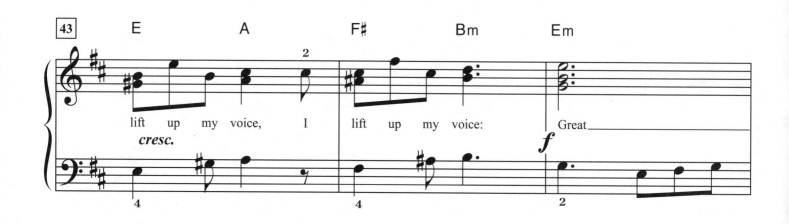

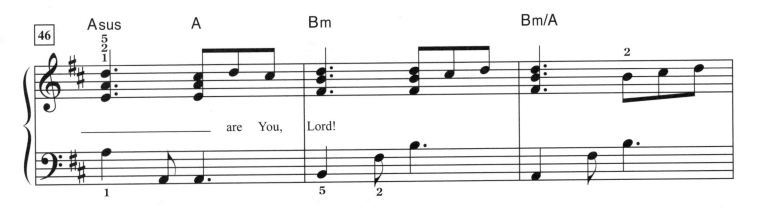

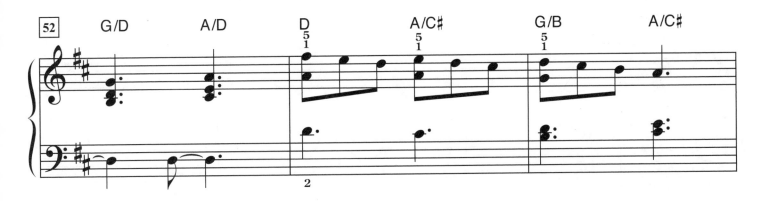

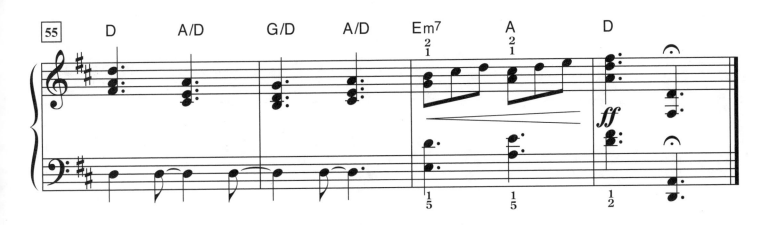

HALLELUJAH

(Your Love Is Amazing)

Words and Music by
Brenton Brown and Brian Doerksen
Arranged by Carol Tornquist

1. Your love is a-maz-

© 2000 VINEYARD SONGS (UK/EIRE)
All Rights in North America Administered by MUSIC SERVICES, INC.
All Rights Reserved   Used by Permission

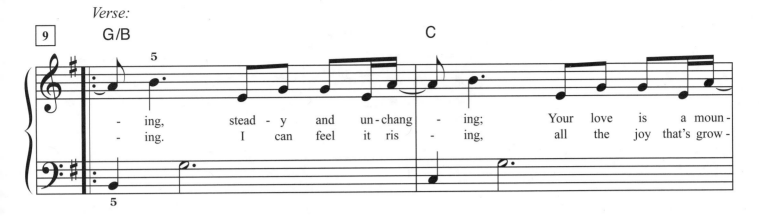

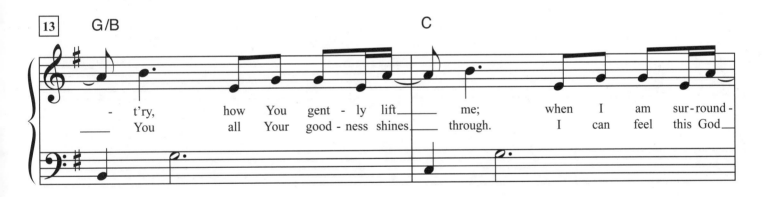

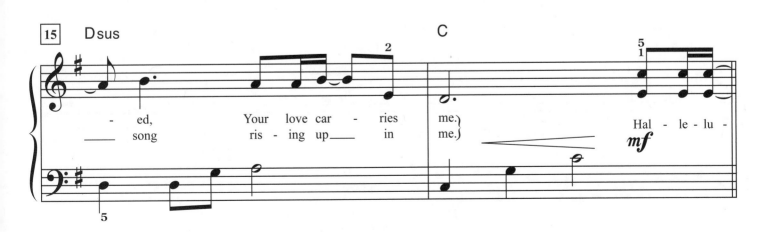

Chorus:

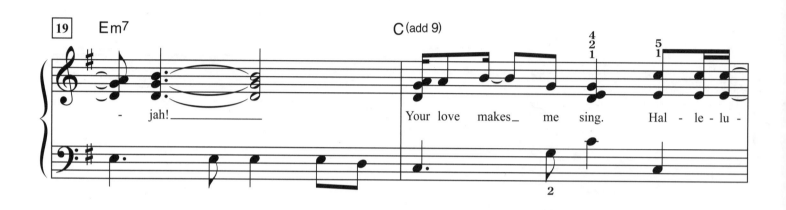

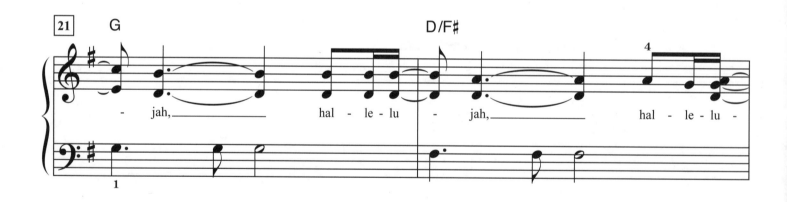

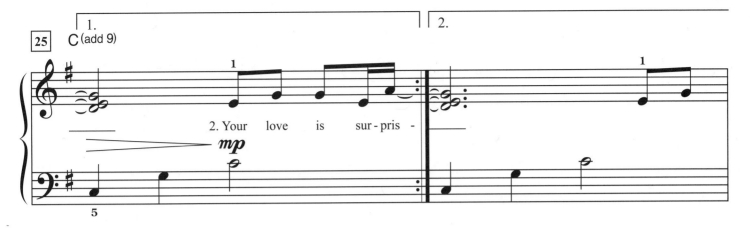

2. Your love is sur-pris -

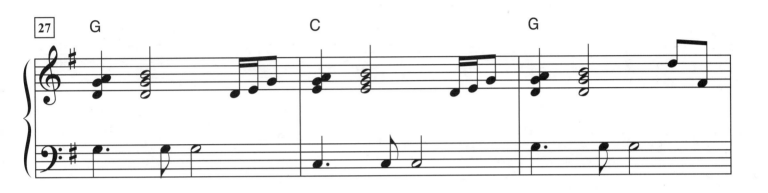

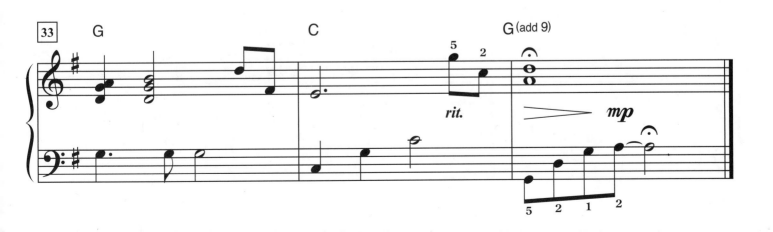

HE KNOWS MY NAME

Words and Music by Tommy Walker
Arranged by Carol Tornquist

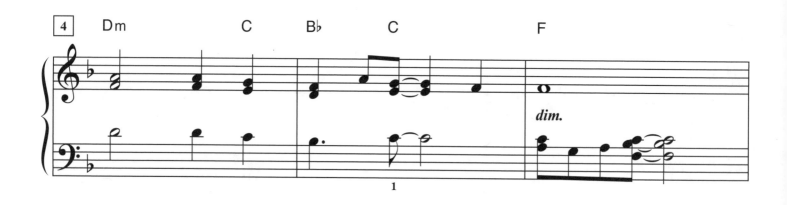

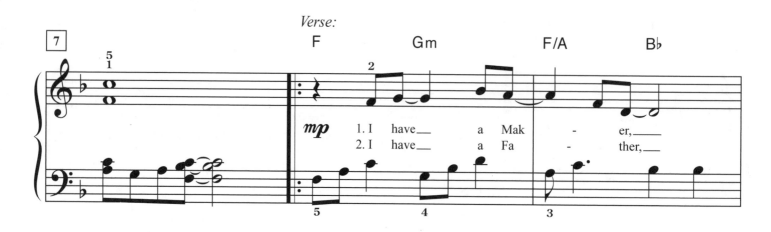

© 1996 DOULOS PUBLISHING
All Rights Administered by MARANATHA! MUSIC
All Rights Reserved   Used by Permission

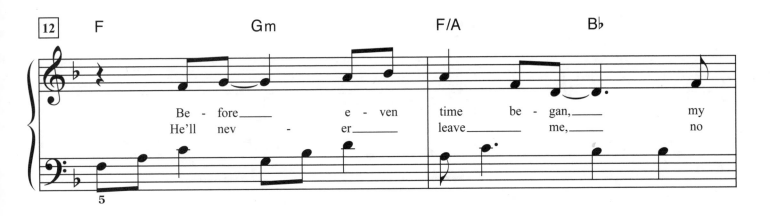

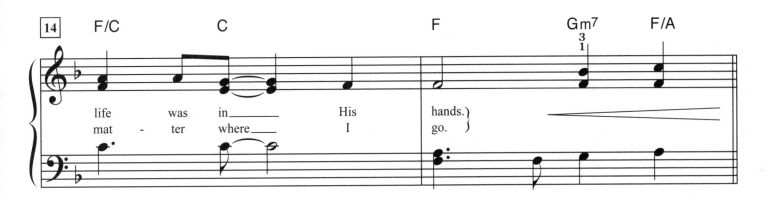

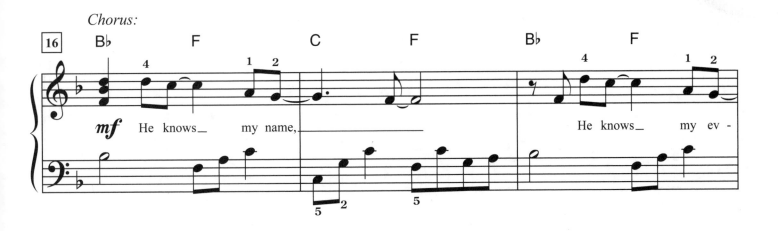

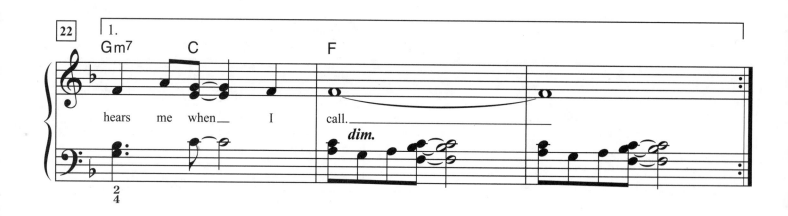

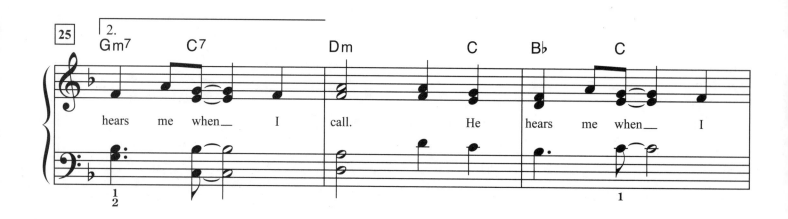

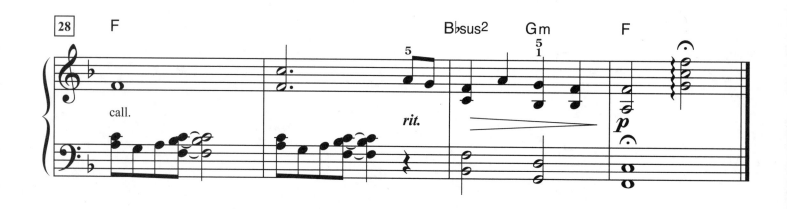

THE HEART OF WORSHIP

Words and Music by Matt Redman
Arranged by Carol Tornquist

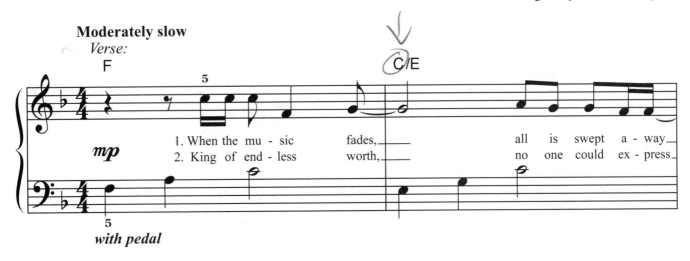

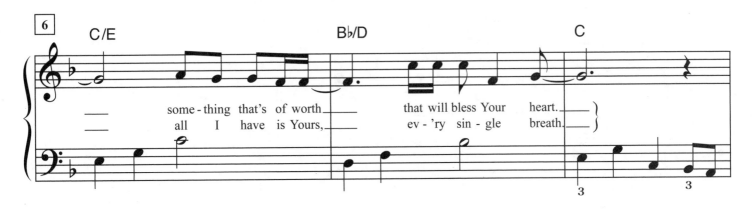

© 1999 THANKYOU MUSIC (PRS) (Administered worldwide at EMICMGPublishing.com
excluding Europe which is administered by kingswaysongs.com)
All Rights Reserved   Used by Permission

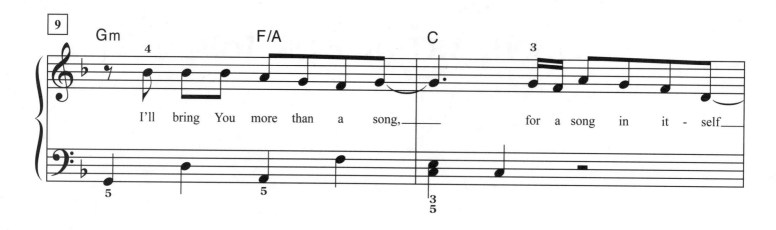

I'll bring You more than a song, _____ for a song in it - self _____

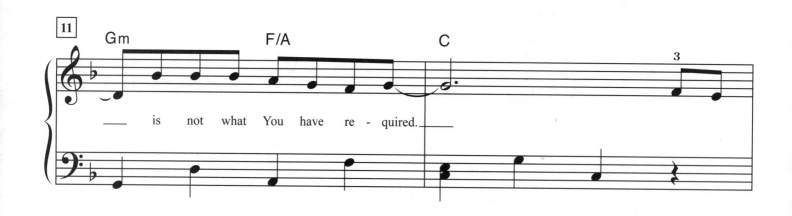

_____ is not what You have re - quired. _____

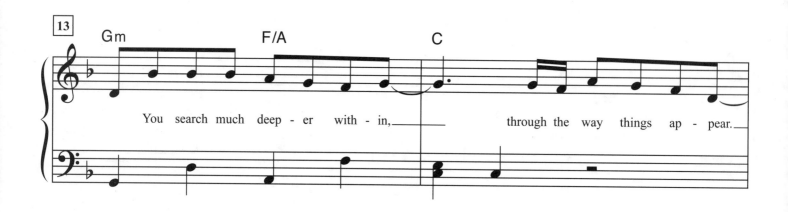

You search much deep - er with - in, _____ through the way things ap - pear. _____

Chorus:

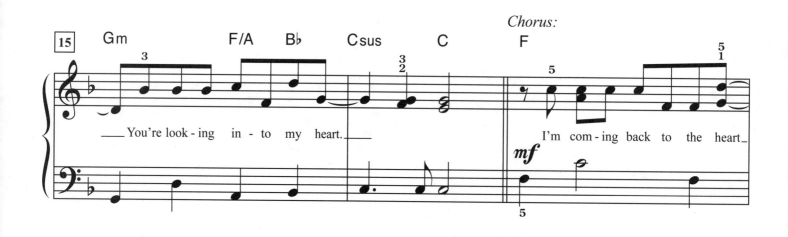

_____ You're look - ing in - to my heart. _____ I'm com - ing back to the heart _____

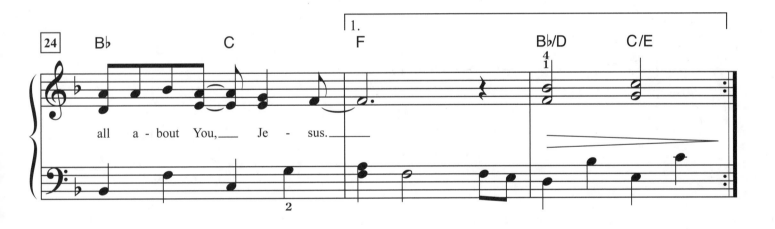

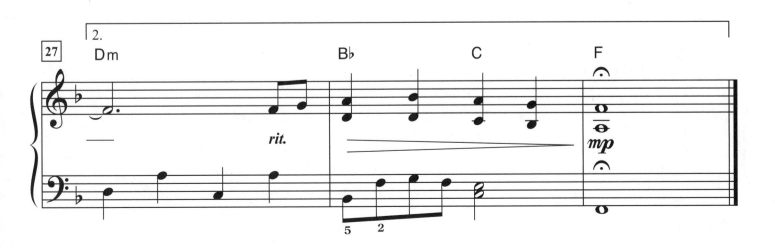

HERE I AM TO WORSHIP

Words and Music by Tim Hughes
Arranged by Carol Tornquist

© 2001 THANKYOU MUSIC (PRS) (Administered worldwide at EMICMGPublishing.com excluding Europe which is administered by kingswaysongs.com)
All Rights Reserved   Used by Permission

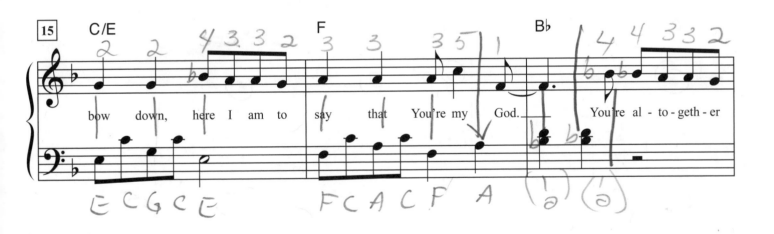

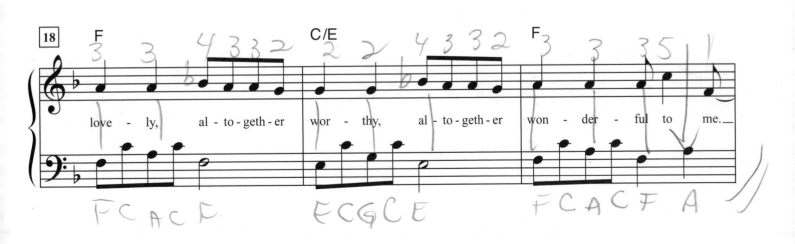

74

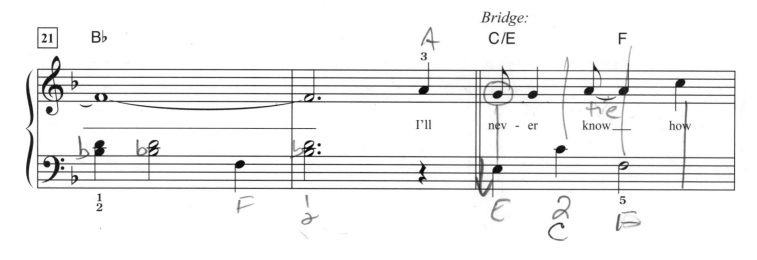

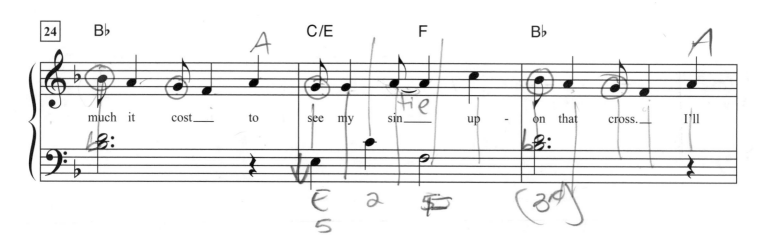

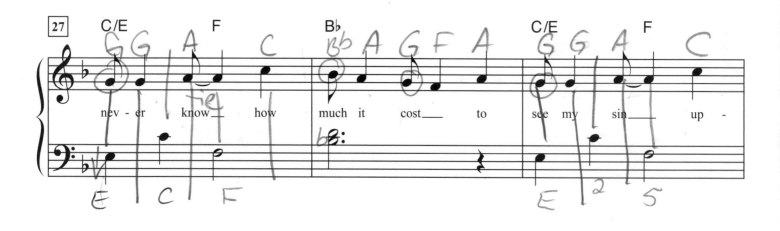

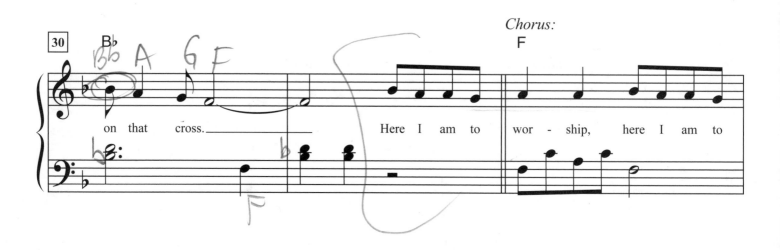

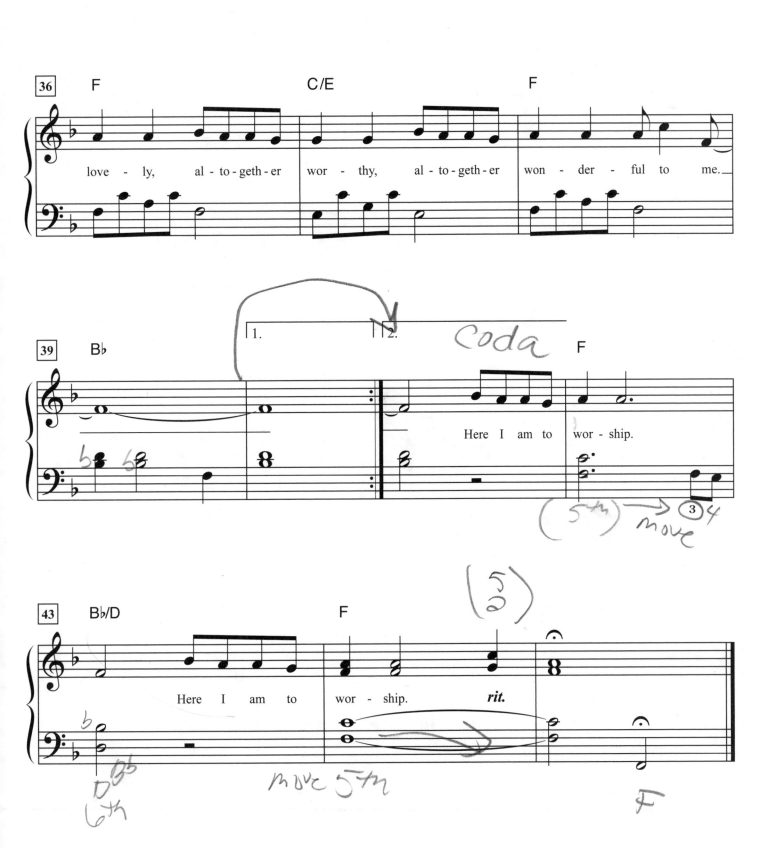

HOLY, HOLY, HOLY

Words and Music by Gary Oliver
Arranged by Carol Tornquist

© 1991 CMI-HP PUBLISHING
All Rights Administered by WORD MUSIC, LLC
All Rights Reserved   Used by Permission

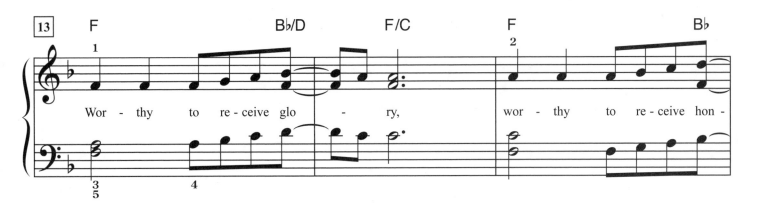

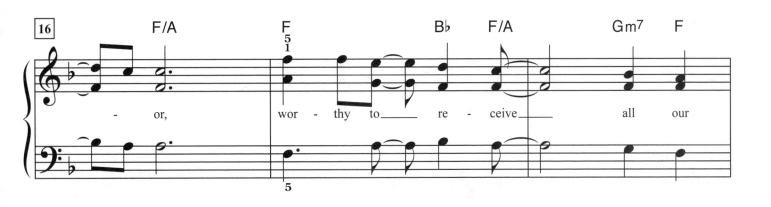

Chorus:

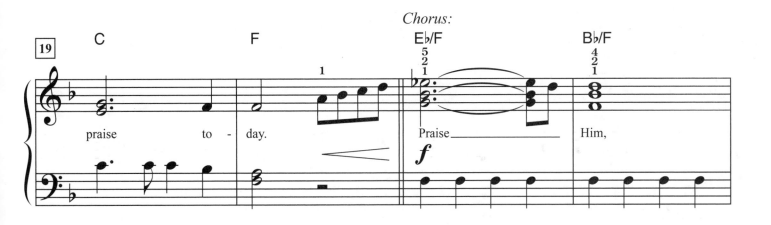

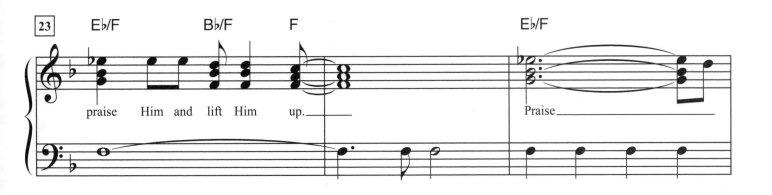

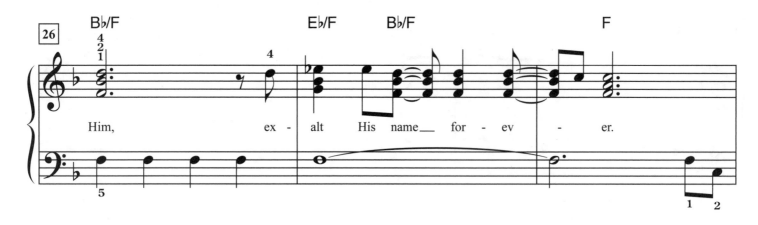

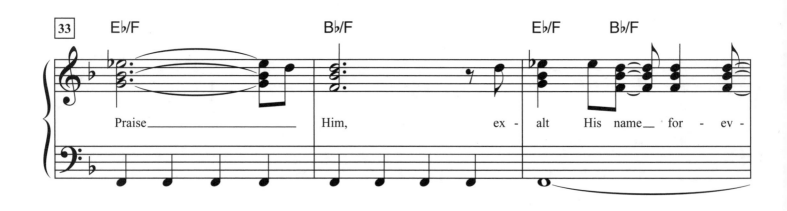

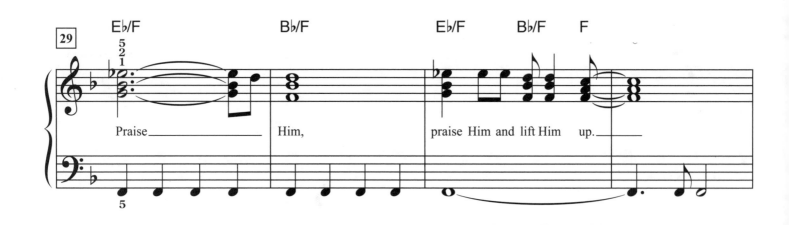

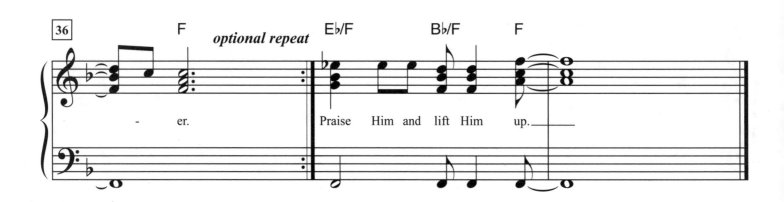

HOLY IS THE LORD

Words and Music by
Chris Tomlin and Louie Giglio
Arranged by Carol Tornquist

Moderately, with reverence

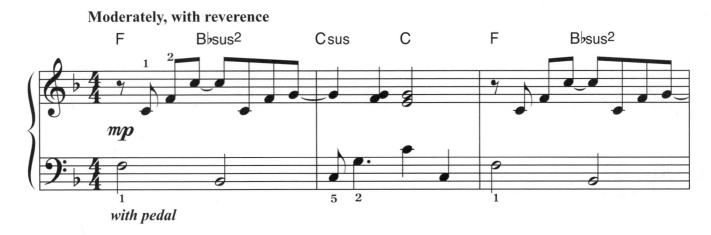

Verse:

We stand and lift up our hands, ___ for the joy ___

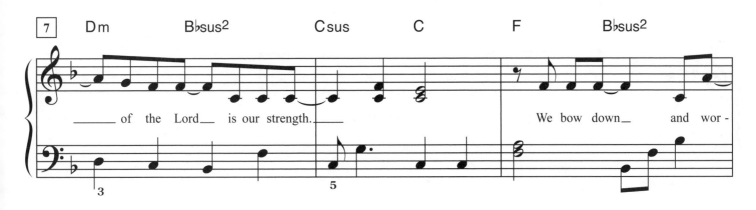

___ of the Lord ___ is our strength. ___ We bow down ___ and wor-

© 2003 WORSHIPTOGETHER.COM SONGS and SIXSTEPS MUSIC
All Rights Administered at EMICMGPublishing.com
All Rights Reserved   Used by Permission

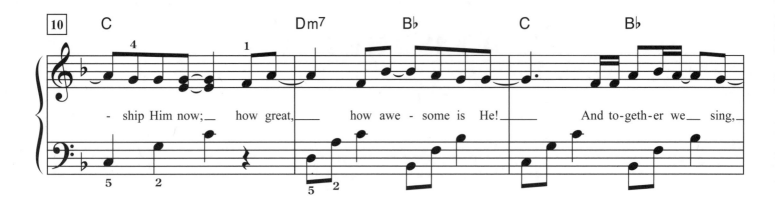

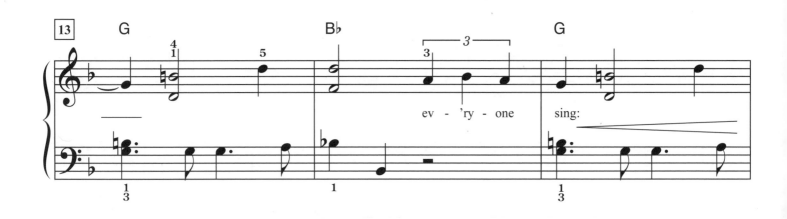

Chorus:

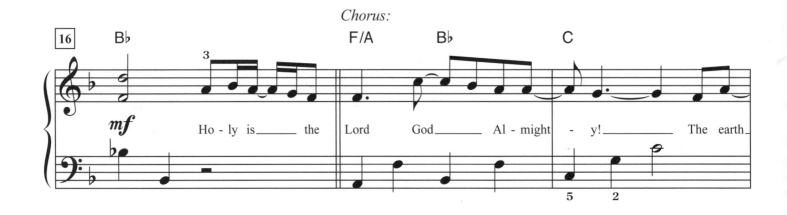

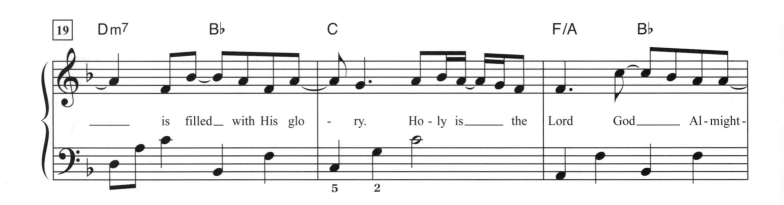

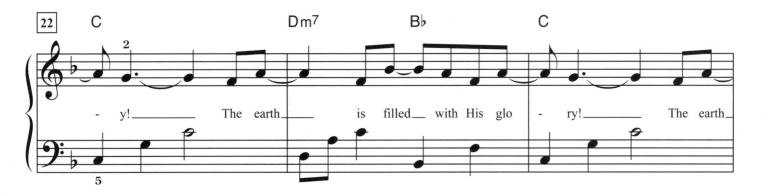

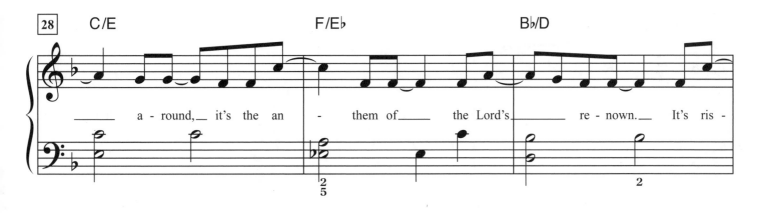

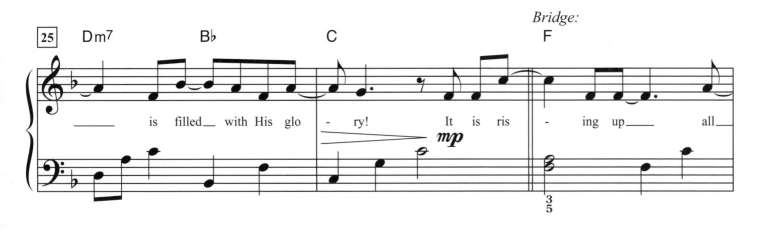

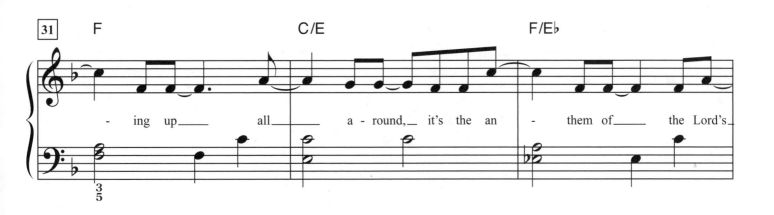

34 Bb/D — Bb — G

_____ re - nown.___ And to-geth-er we sing,___

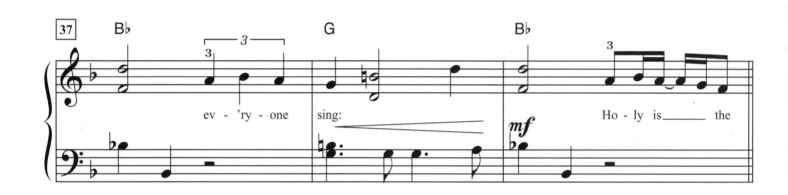

37 Bb — G — Bb

ev - 'ry - one sing: _mf_ Ho - ly is_____ the

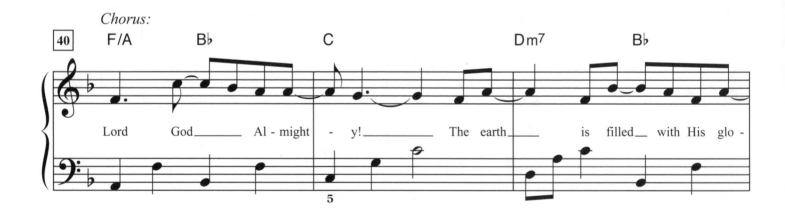

Chorus:

40 F/A — Bb — C — Dm7 — Bb

Lord God_____ Al - might - y!_____ The earth_____ is filled_ with His glo -

43 C — Dm7 — Bb — C

- ry! Ho - ly is_____ the Lord God_____ Al - might - y!_____ The earth

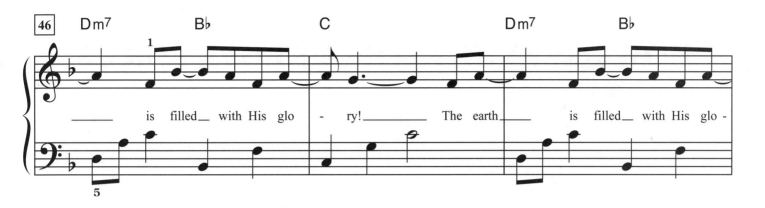

is filled with His glo - ry! The earth is filled with His glo -

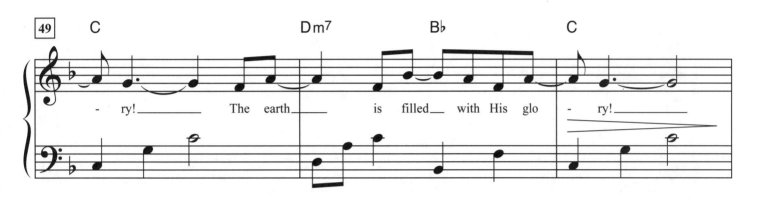

- ry! The earth is filled with His glo - ry!

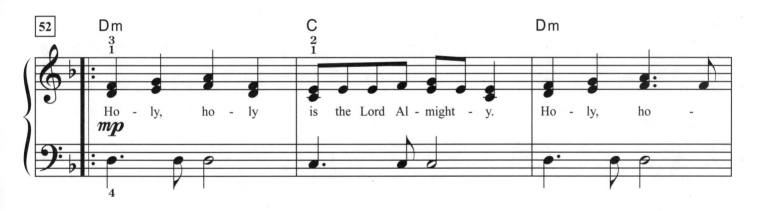

Ho - ly, ho - ly is the Lord Al - might - y. Ho - ly, ho -

mp

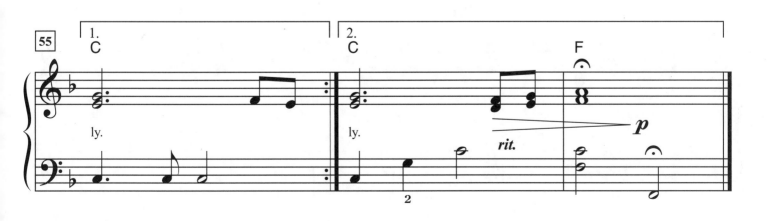

ly. ly. *rit.* *p*

HOW DEEP THE FATHER'S LOVE FOR US

Words and Music by Stuart Townend
Arranged by Carol Tornquist

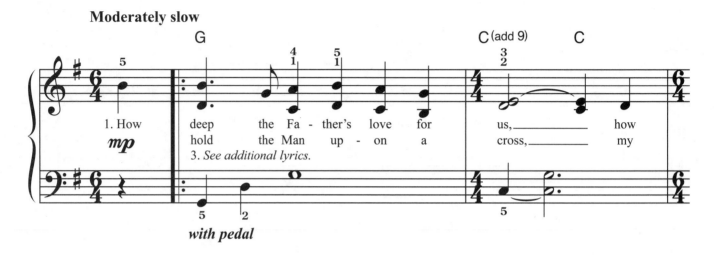

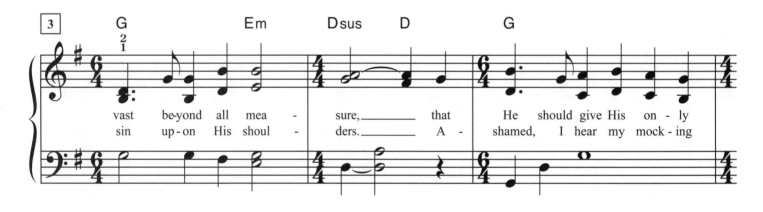

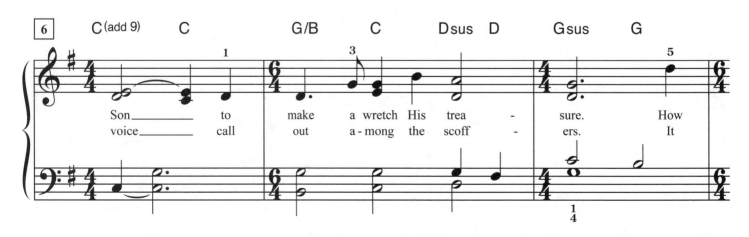

© 1995 THANKYOU MUSIC (PRS) (Administered worldwide at EMICMGPublishing.com
excluding Europe which is administered by kingswaysongs.com)
All Rights Reserved   Used by Permission

Verse 3:
I will not boast in anything: no gifts, no power, no wisdom;
But I will boast in Jesus Christ, His death and resurrection.
Why should I gain from His reward? I cannot give an answer.
But this I know with all my heart: His wounds have paid my ransom.

HOW GREAT IS OUR GOD

Words and Music by
Jesse Reeves, Chris Tomlin and Ed Cash
Arranged by Carol Tornquist

© 2004 WORSHIPTOGETHER.COM SONGS, SIXSTEPS MUSIC and ALLETROP MUSIC
All Rights for WORSHIPTOGETHER.COM SONGS and SIXSTEPS MUSIC Administered at EMICMGPublishing.com
All Rights for ALLETROP MUSIC Administered by MUSIC SERVICES, INC.
All Rights Reserved   Used by Permission

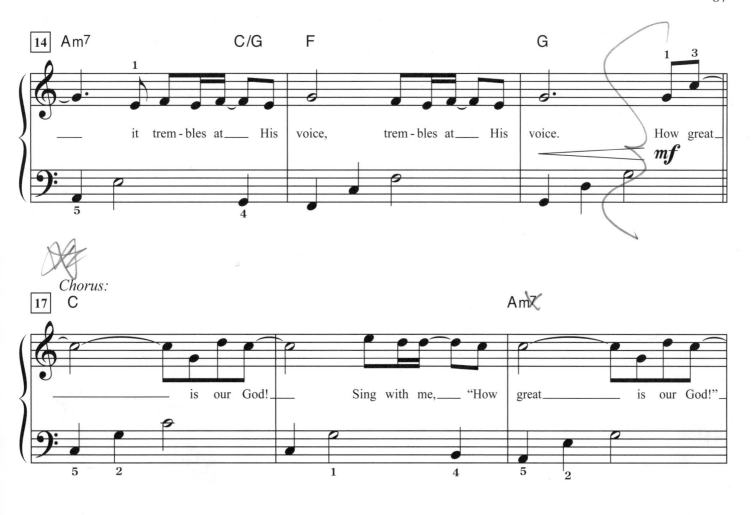

Chorus:

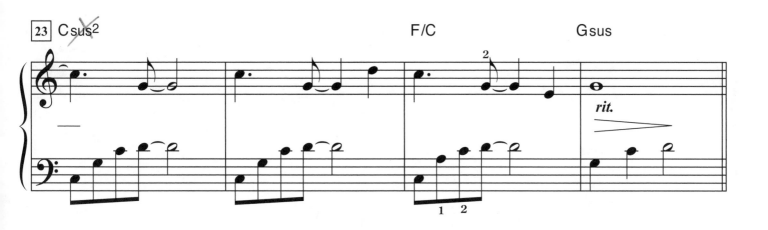

Chorus:

is our God! Sing with me, "How great_____ is our God!"

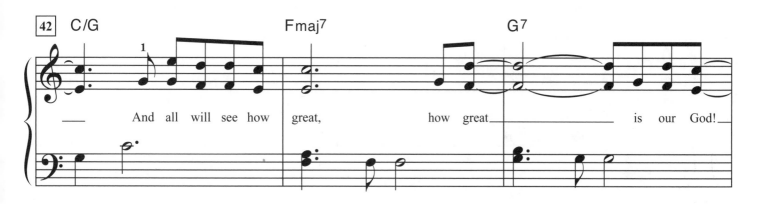

_____ And all will see how great, how great_____ is our God!

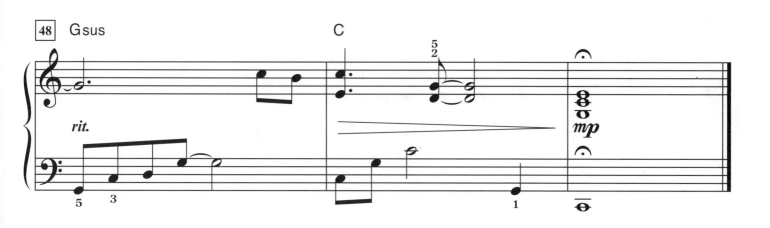

I COULD SING OF YOUR LOVE FOREVER

Words and Music by Martin Smith
Arranged by Carol Tornquist

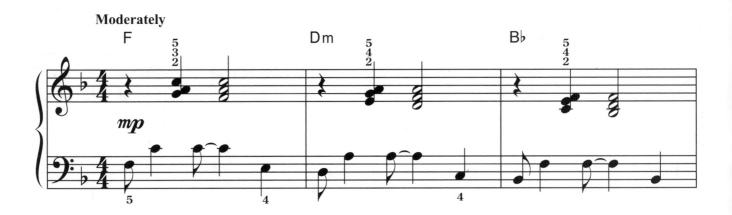

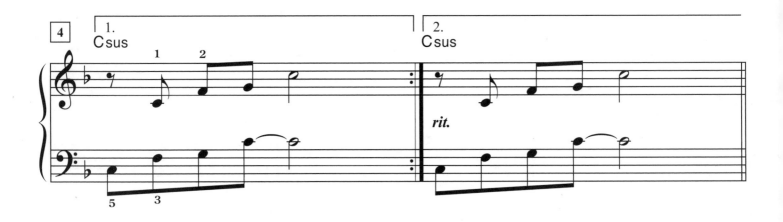

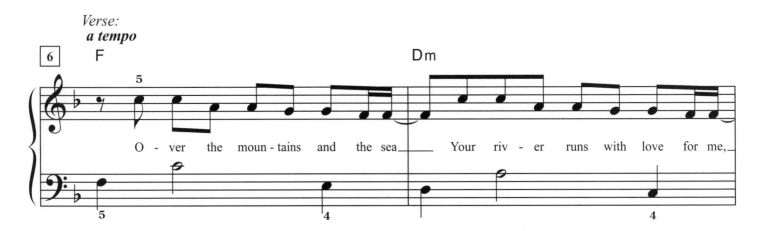

O - ver the moun - tains and the sea___ Your riv - er runs with love for me,

© 1994 CURIOUS? MUSIC UK (PRS)
All Rights in the U.S. and Canada Administered at EMICMGPublishing.com
All Rights Reserved   Used by Permission

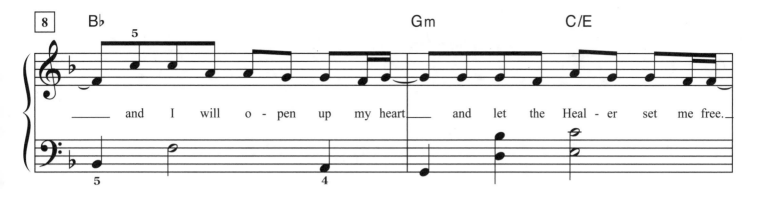

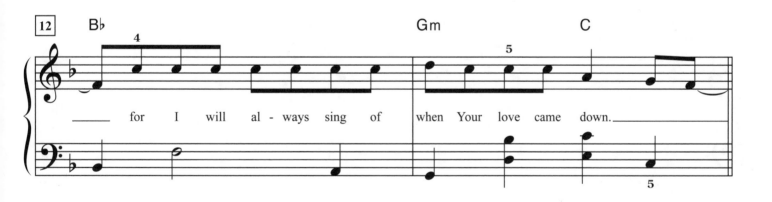

Chorus:

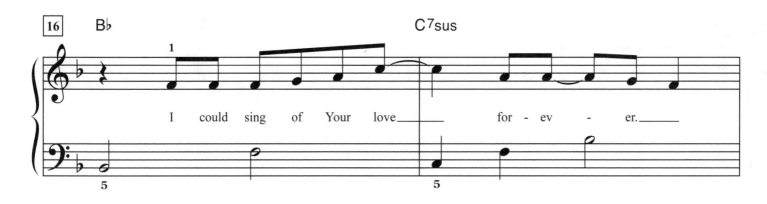

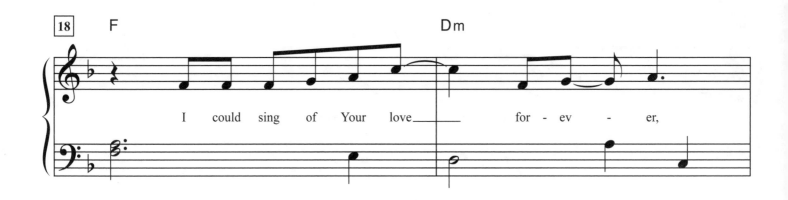

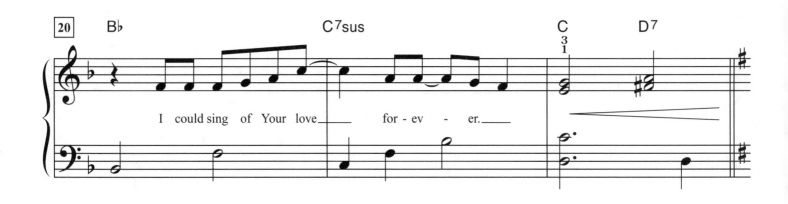

I could sing of Your love____ for - ev - er.____

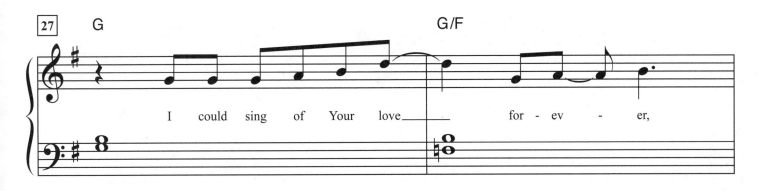

I could sing of Your love____ for - ev - er,

I could sing of Your love.____

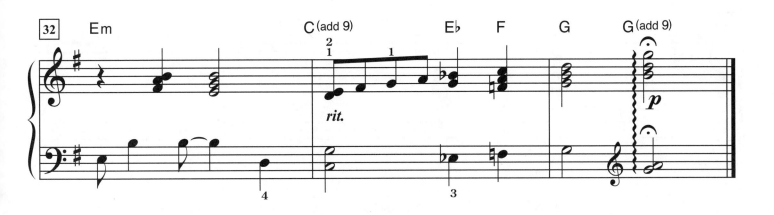

HOSANNA

(Praise Is Rising)

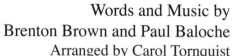

Words and Music by
Brenton Brown and Paul Baloche
Arranged by Carol Tornquist

© 2006 THANKYOU MUSIC (PRS) (Administered worldwide at EMICMGPublishing.com)
excluding Europe which is administered by kingswaysongs.com) and INTEGRITY'S HOSANNA! (Administered at EMICMGPublishing.com)
All Rights Reserved   Used by Permission

I LIFT MY EYES UP

(Psalm 121)

Words and Music by Brian Doerksen
Arranged by Carol Tornquist

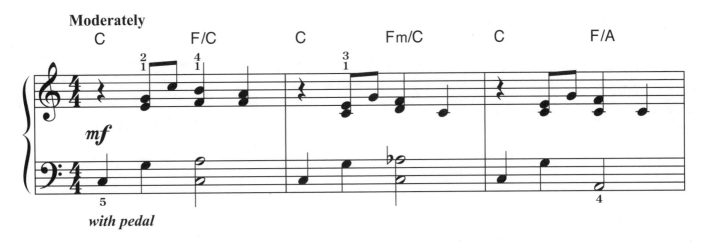

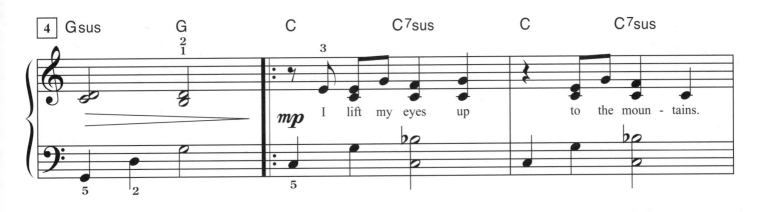

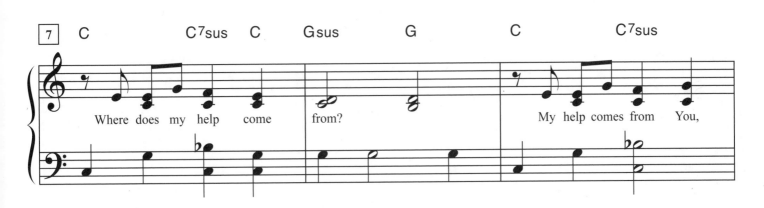

© 1990 VINEYARD SONGS (CANADA)/ION PUBLISHING (SOCAN)
Administered in North America by MUSIC SERVICES, INC. on behalf of VINEYARD MUSIC USA
All Rights Reserved   Used by Permission

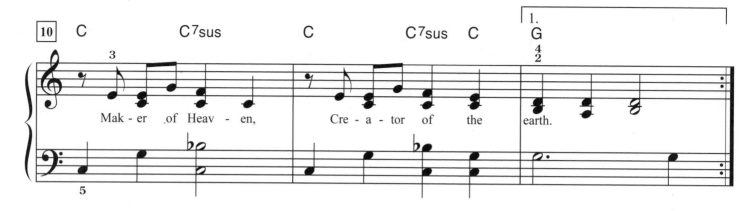

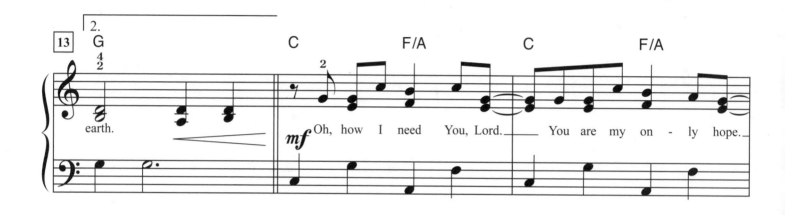

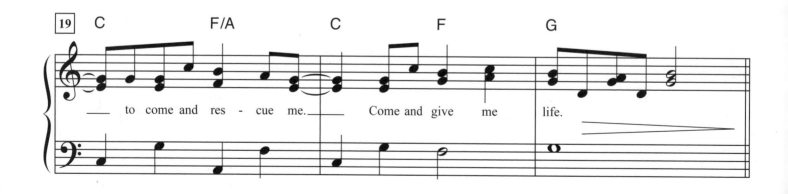

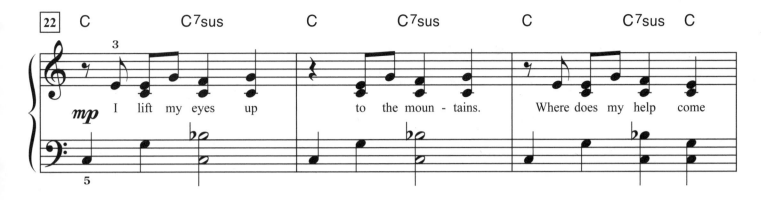

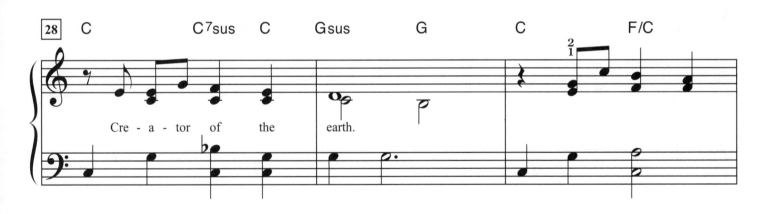

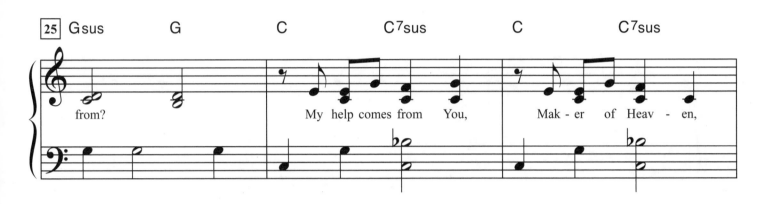

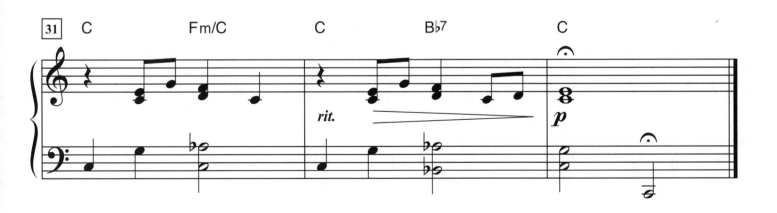

IN CHRIST ALONE

(My Hope Is Found)

Words and Music by
Stuart Townend and Keith Getty
Arranged by Carol Tornquist

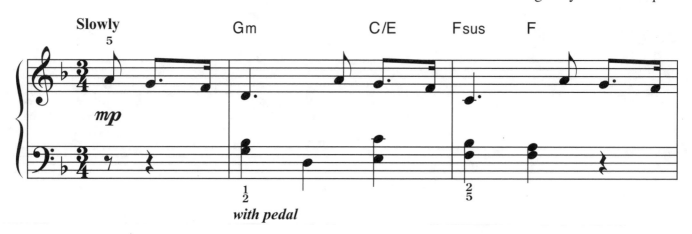

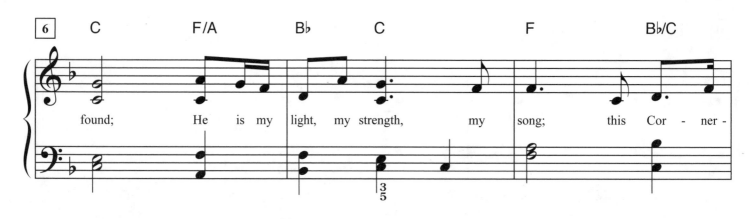

© 2002 THANKYOU MUSIC (PRS) (Administered worldwide at EMICMGPublishing.com
excluding Europe which is administered by kingswaysongs.com)
All Rights Reserved   Used by Permission

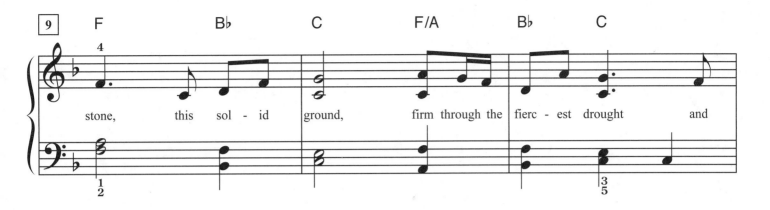

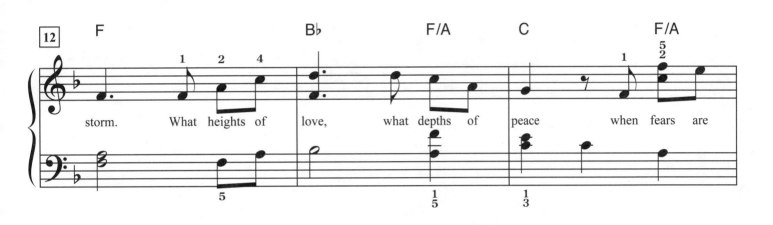

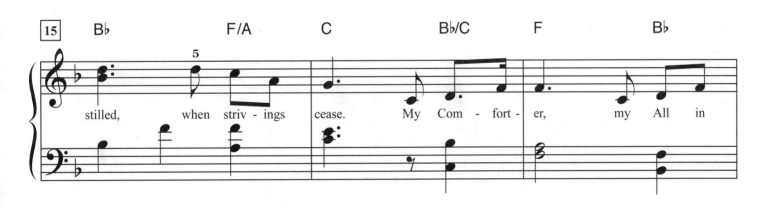

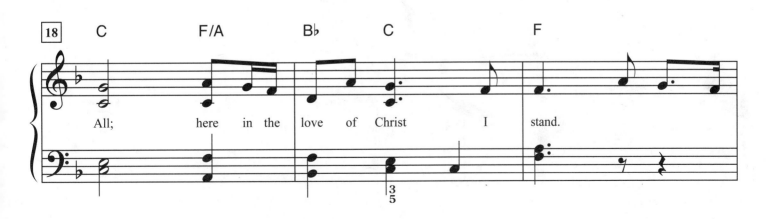

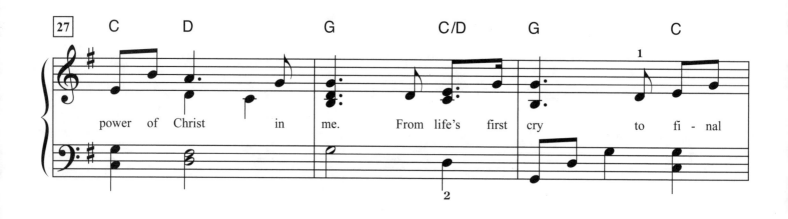

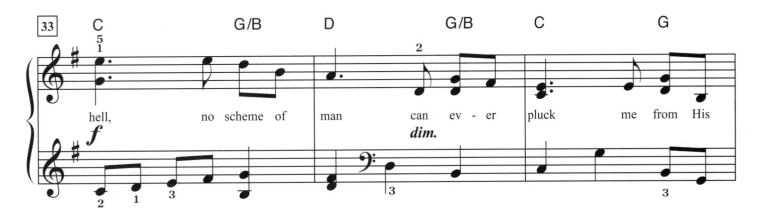

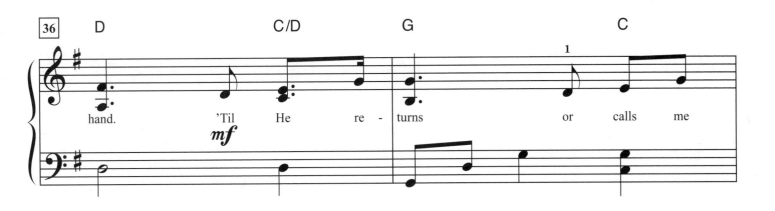

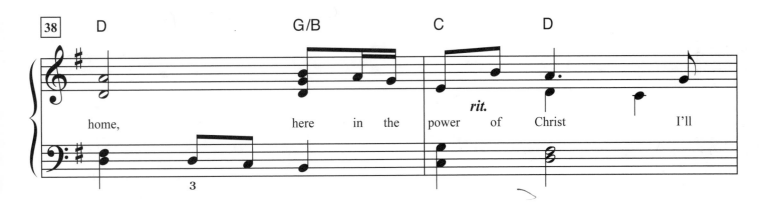

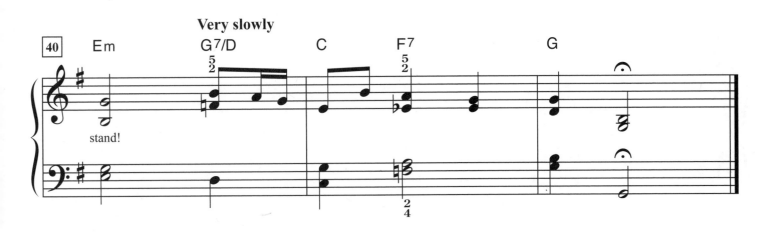

IN THE SECRET

Words and Music by Andy Park
Arranged by Carol Tornquist

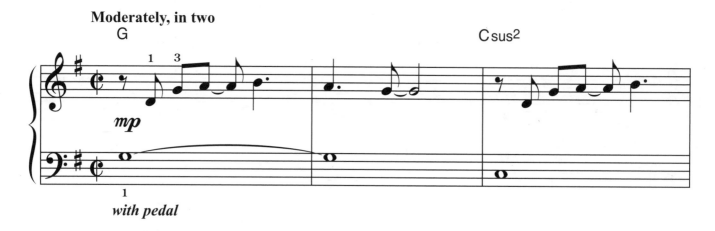

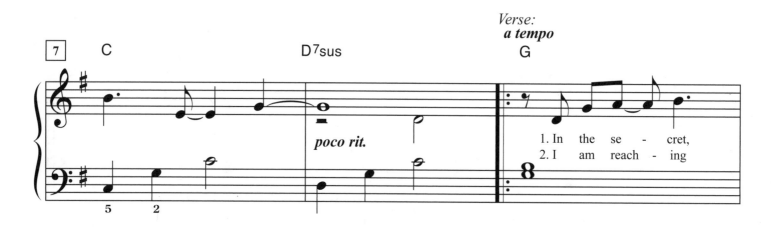

© 1995 MERCY/VINEYARD PUBLISHING
All Rights for North America Administered by MUSIC SERVICES, INC. on behalf of VINEYARD MUSIC USA
All Rights Reserved   Used by Permission

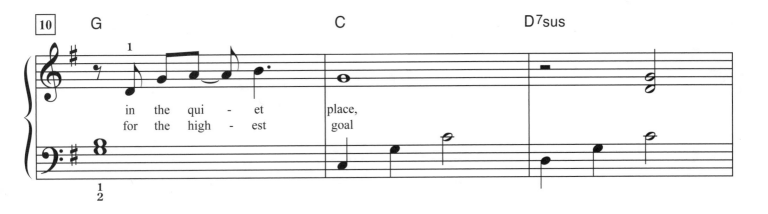

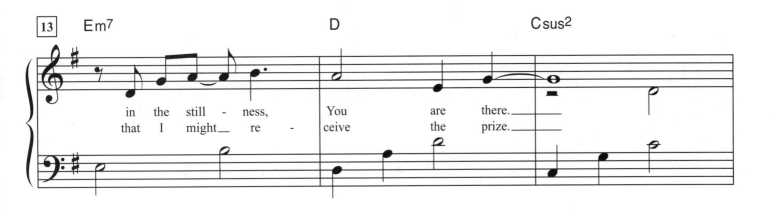

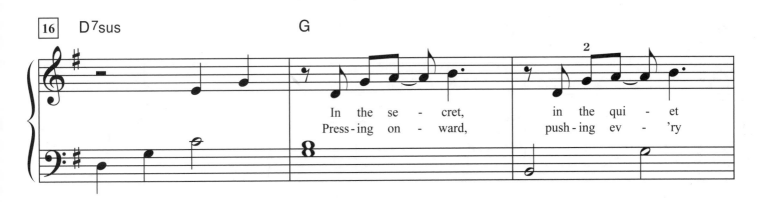

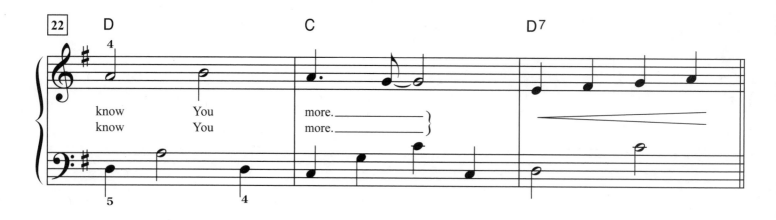

22 | D | C | D7

know   You   more.
know   You   more.

Chorus:

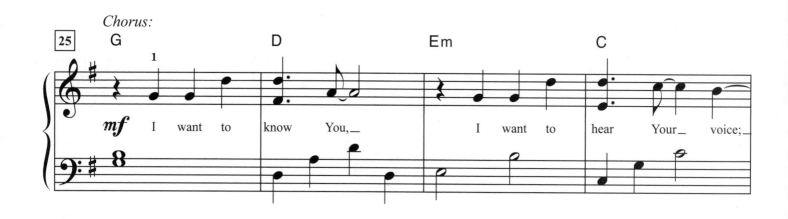

25 | G | D | Em | C

mf I want to know You,   I want to hear Your voice;

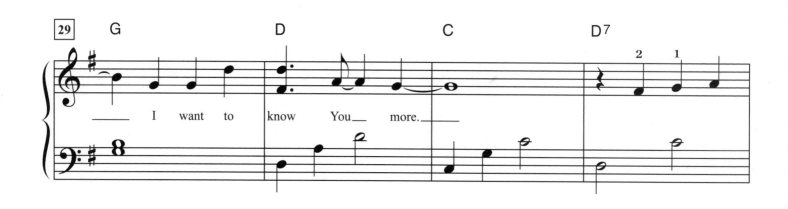

29 | G | D | C | D7

I want to know You more.

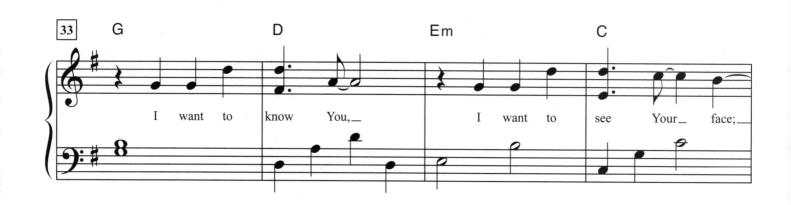

33 | G | D | Em | C

I want to know You,   I want to see Your face;

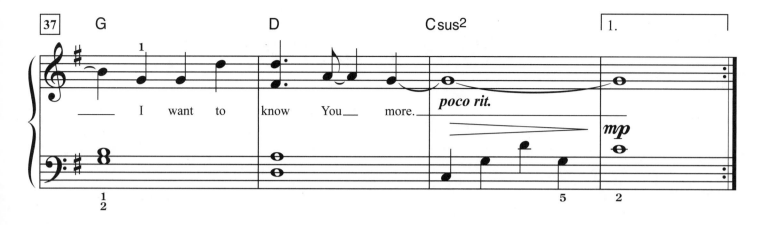

I want to know You more.

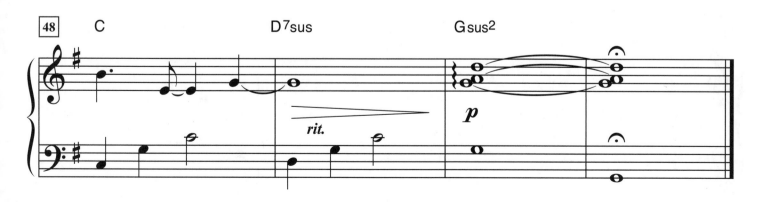

INDESCRIBABLE

Words and Music by
Jesse Reeves and Laura Story
Arranged by Carol Tornquist

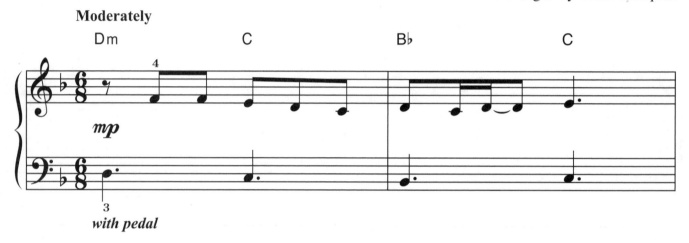

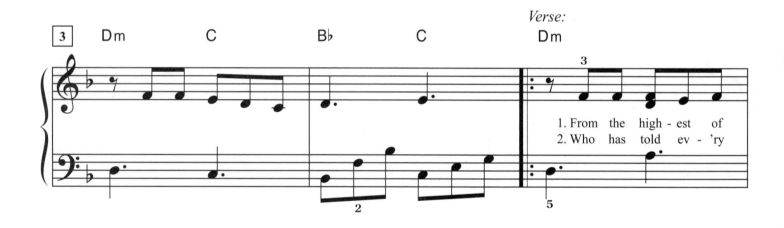

© 2004 WORSHIPTOGETHER.COM SONGS, SIXSTEPS MUSIC and GLEANING PUBLISHING
All Rights Administered at EMICMGPublishing.com
All Rights Reserved   Used by Permission

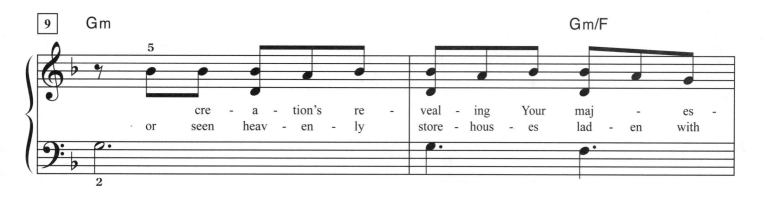

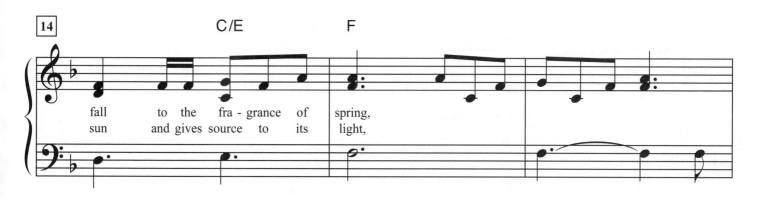

Chorus:

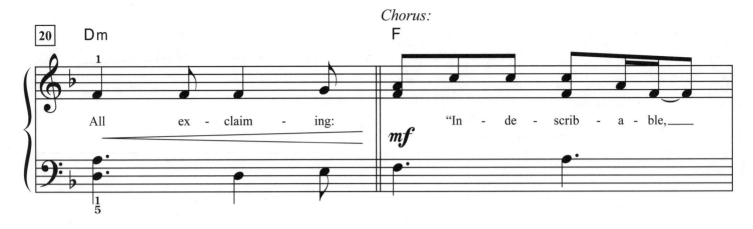

20 Dm / F

All ex - claim - ing: "In - de - scrib - a - ble,___

mf

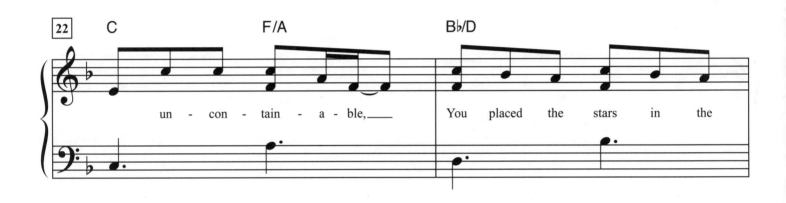

22 C / F/A / B♭/D

un - con - tain - a - ble,___ You placed the stars in the

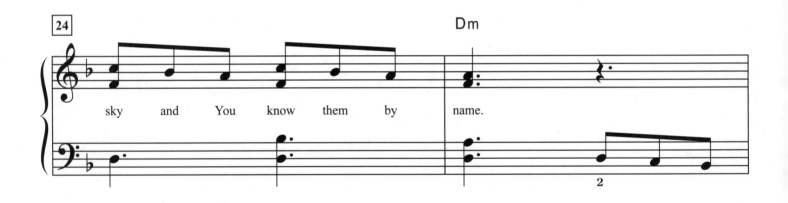

24 Dm

sky and You know them by name.

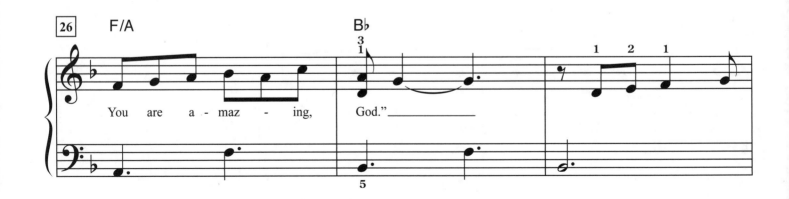

26 F/A / B♭

You are a - maz - ing, God."___

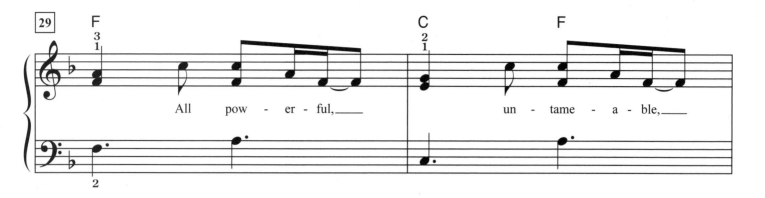

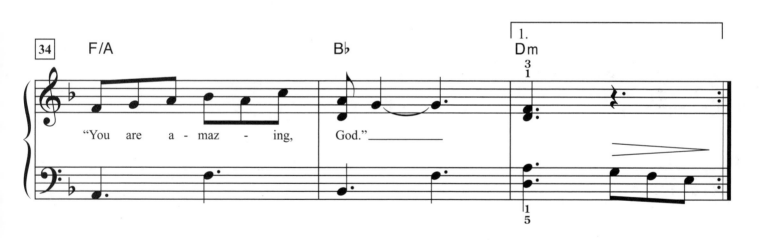

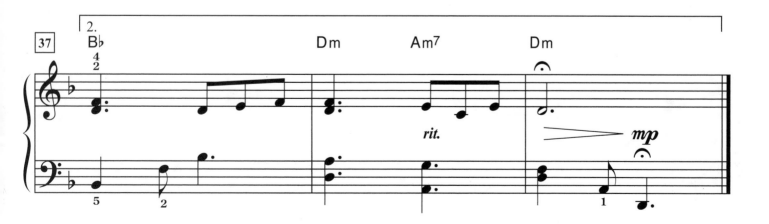

I LOVE YOU, LORD

Words and Music by Laurie Klein
Arranged by Carol Tornquist

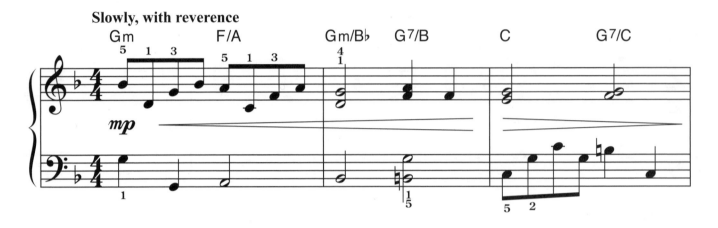

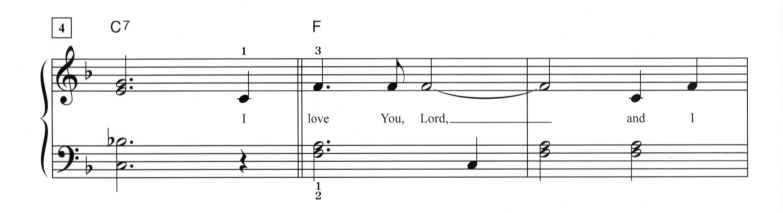

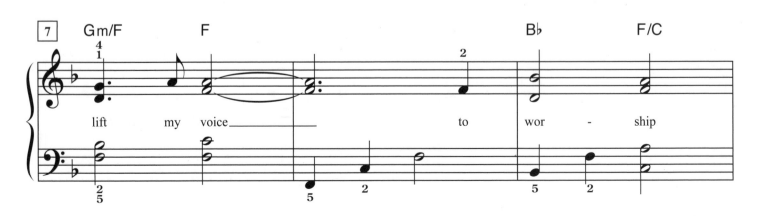

© 1978 HOUSE OF MERCY MUSIC
All Rights Administered by MARANATHA! MUSIC
All Rights Reserved   Used by Permission

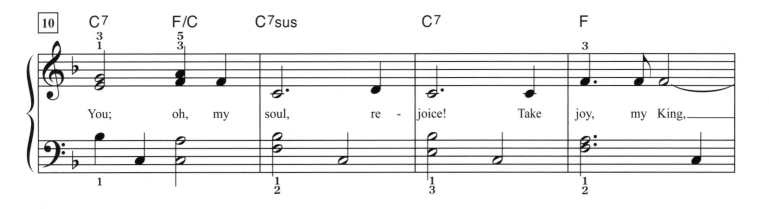

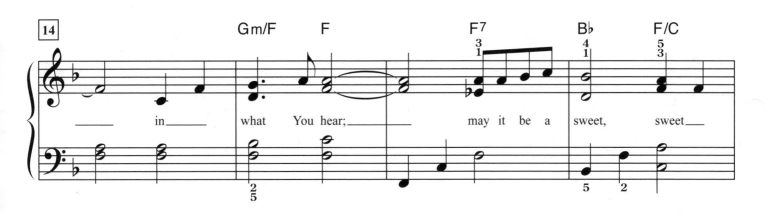

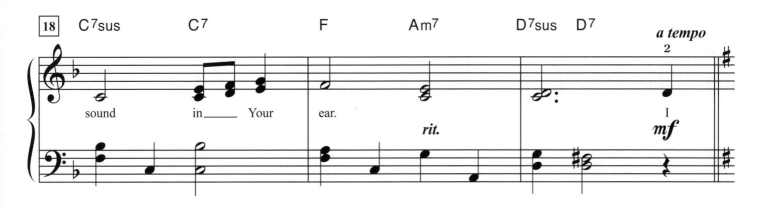

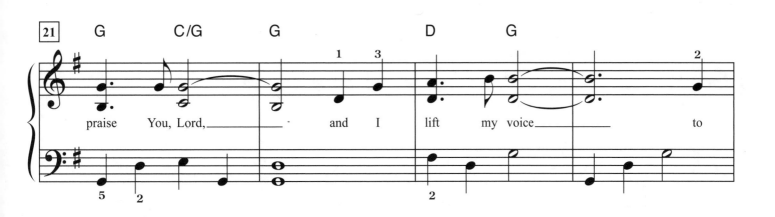

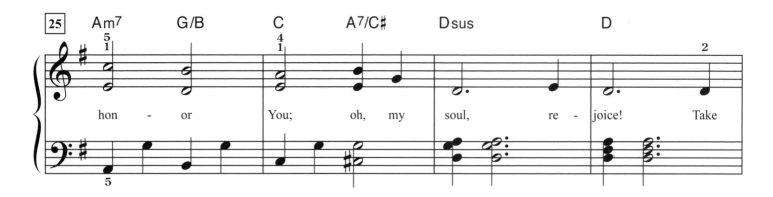

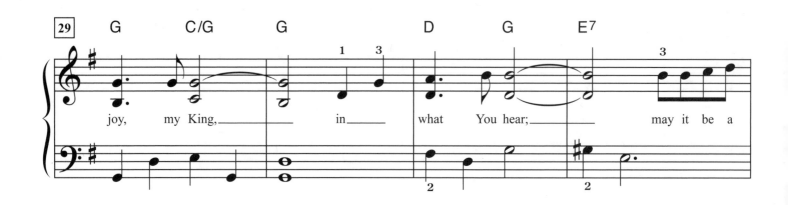

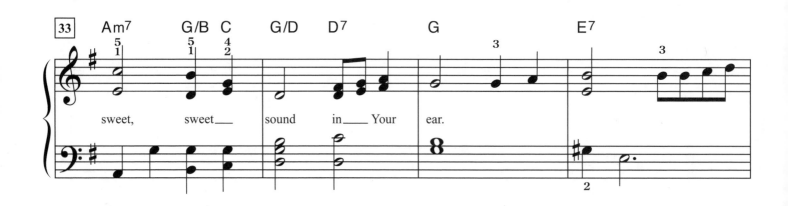

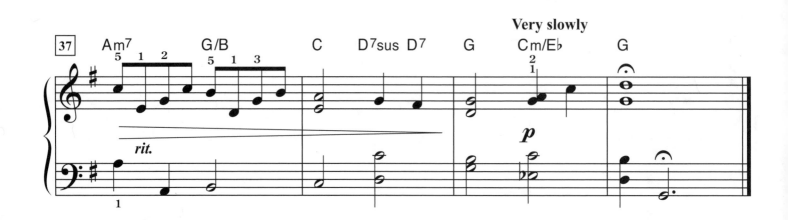

JESUS MESSIAH

Words and Music by
Daniel Carson, Chris Tomlin, Ed Cash and Jesse Reeves
Arranged by Carol Tornquist

© 2008 WORSHIPTOGETHER.COM SONGS, SIXSTEPS MUSIC, VAMOS PUBLISHING and ALLETROP MUSIC
All Rights for WORSHIPTOGETHER.COM SONGS, SIXSTEPS MUSIC and VAMOS PUBLISHING
Administered at EMICMGPublishing.com
All Rights for ALLETROP MUSIC Administered by MUSIC SERVICES, INC.
All Rights Reserved   Used by Permission

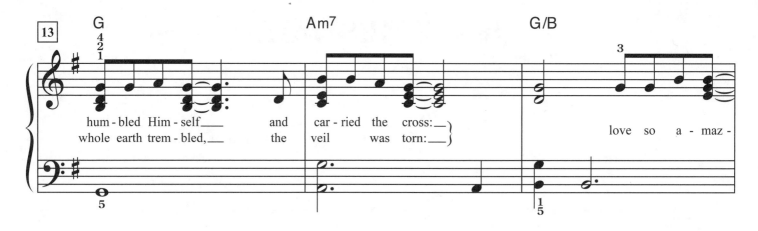

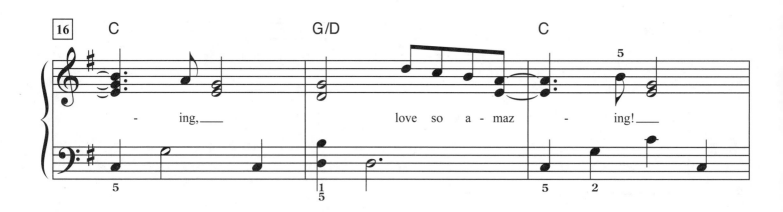

Chorus:

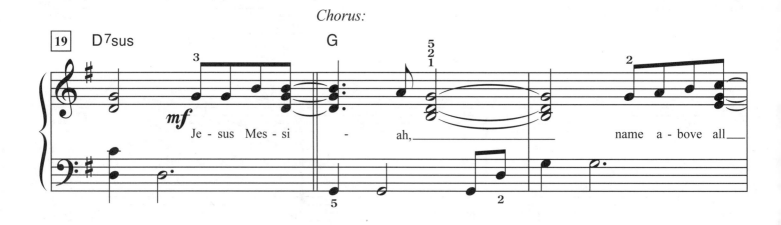

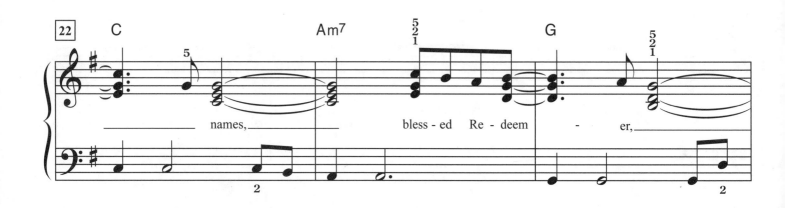

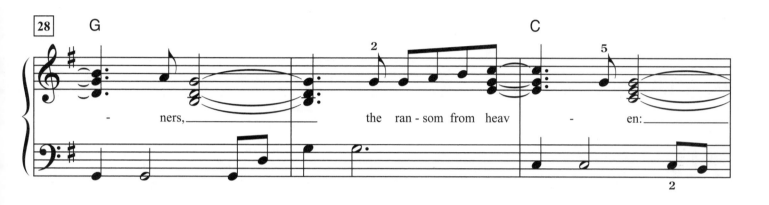

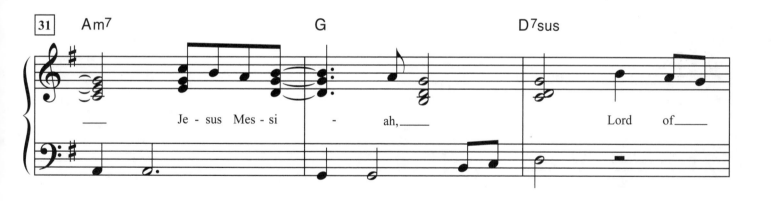

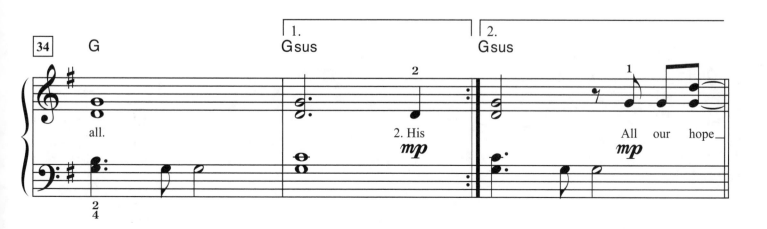

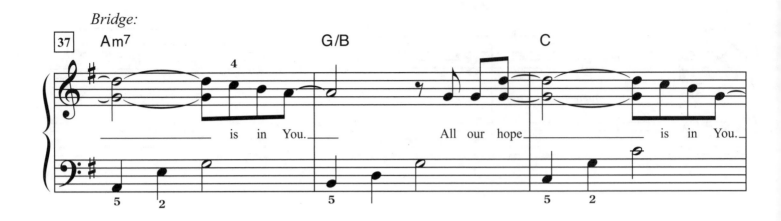

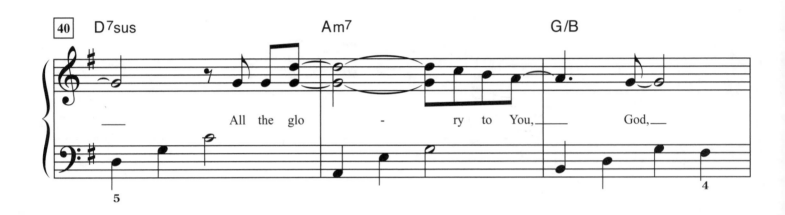

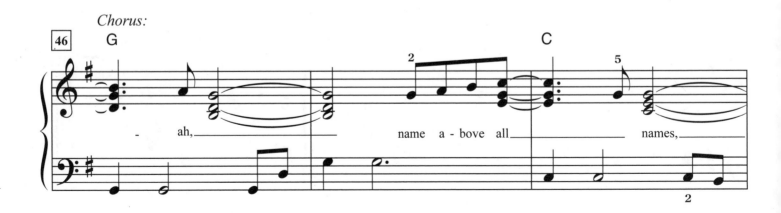

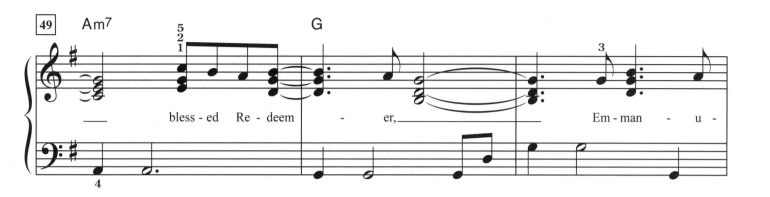

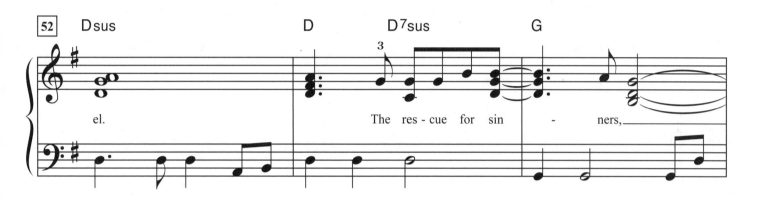

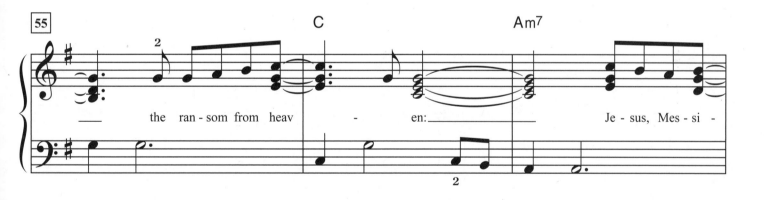

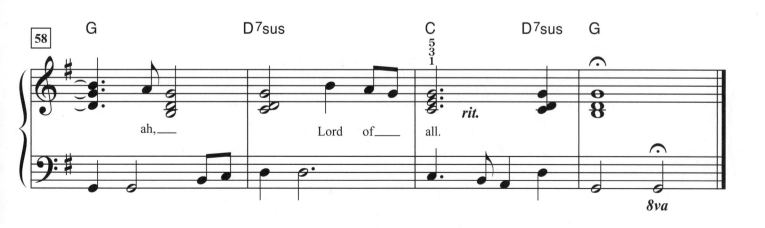

LORD, I LIFT YOUR NAME ON HIGH

Words and Music by Rick Founds
Arranged by Carol Tornquist

© 1989 MARANATHA! PRAISE, INC. (Administered by MUSIC SERVICES, INC.)
All Rights Reserved   Used by Permission

Chorus:

You came from heav - en to earth to show___ the way;___ from the earth___ to the cross,___

___ my debt___ to pay.___ From the cross___ to the grave, ___ from the grave___ to the sky,___

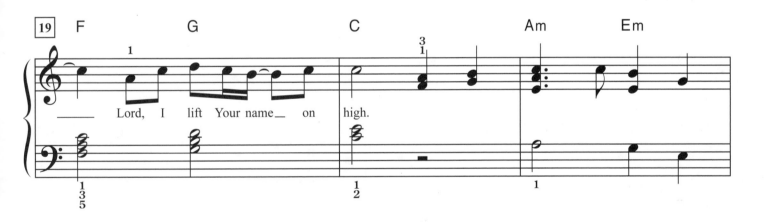

___ Lord, I lift Your name___ on high.

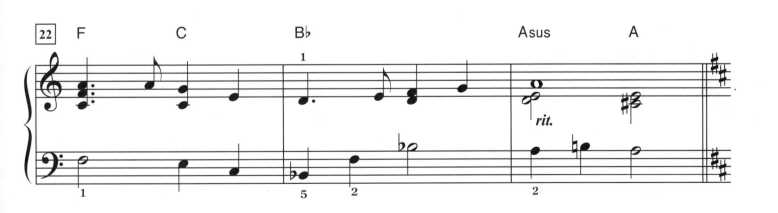

Verse:
a tempo

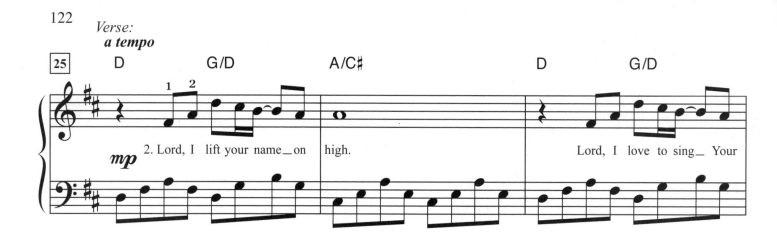

2. Lord, I lift your name_on high. Lord, I love to sing_ Your

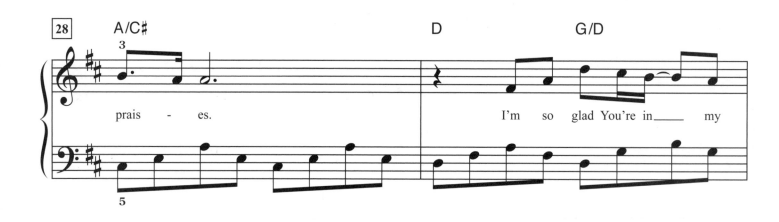

prais - es. I'm so glad You're in____ my

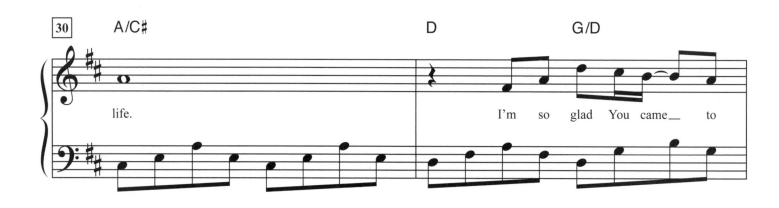

life. I'm so glad You came___ to

Chorus:

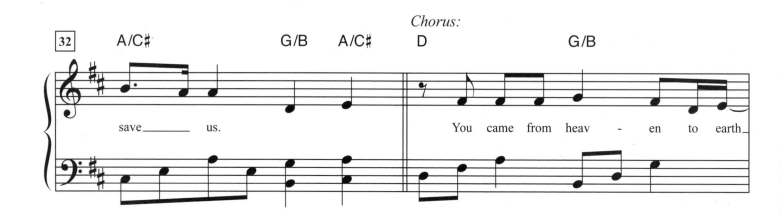

save_____ us. You came from heav - en to earth_

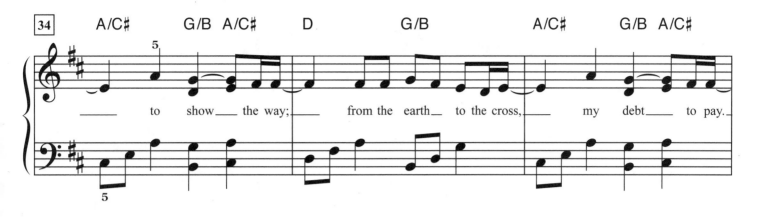

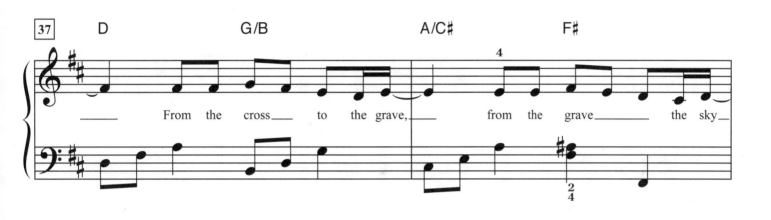

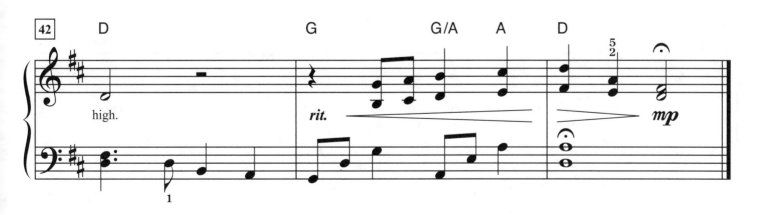

LORD, REIGN IN ME

Words and Music by Brenton Brown
Arranged by Carol Tornquist

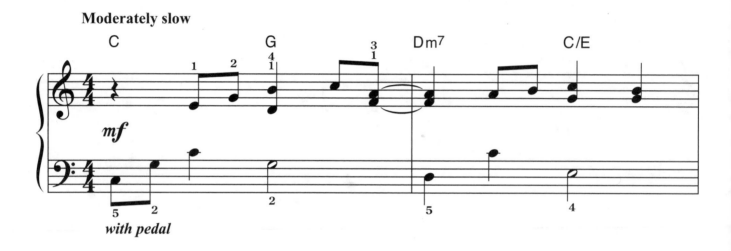

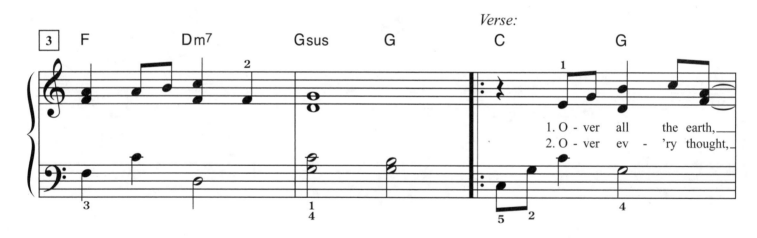

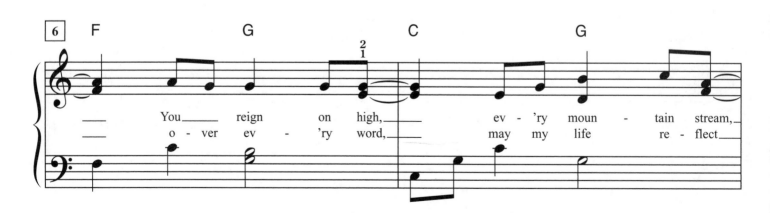

© 1998 VINEYARD SONGS (UK/EIRE) (PRS)
Administered in North America by MUSIC SERVICES, INC.
All Rights Reserved   Used by Permission

125

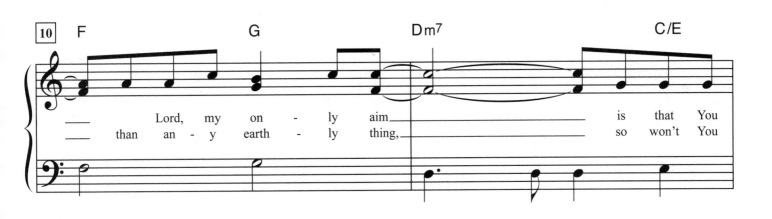

Chorus:

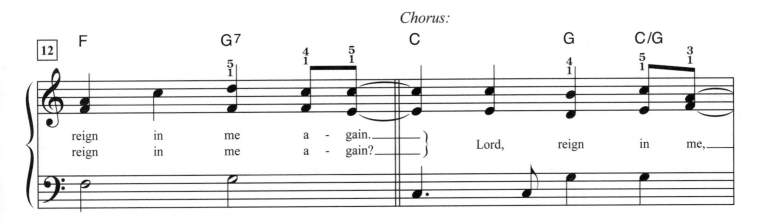

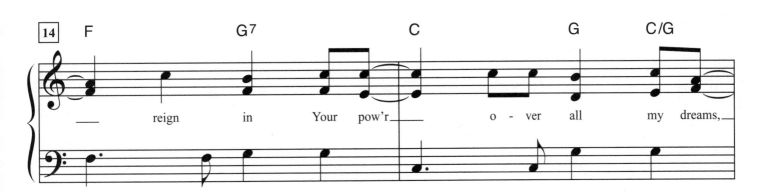

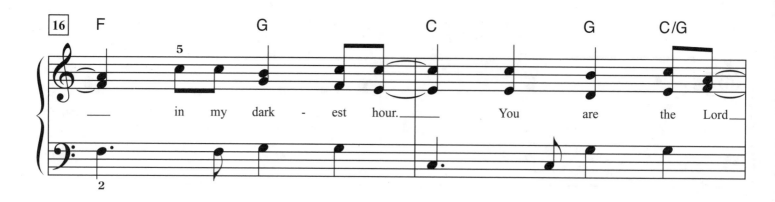

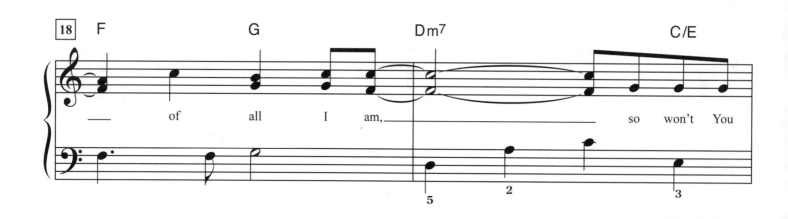

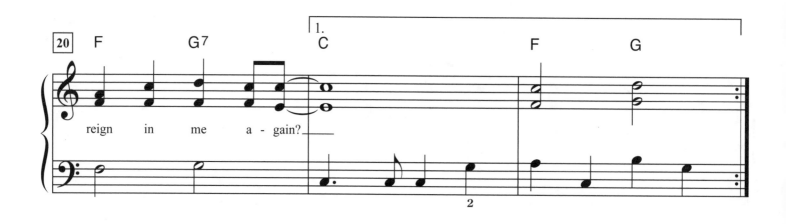

MIGHTY TO SAVE

Words and Music by
Reuben Morgan and Ben Fielding
Arranged by Carol Tornquist

© 2006 HILLSONG PUBLISHING (APRA)
All Rights in the U.S. and Canada Administered at EMICMGPublishing.com
All Rights Reserved   Used by Permission

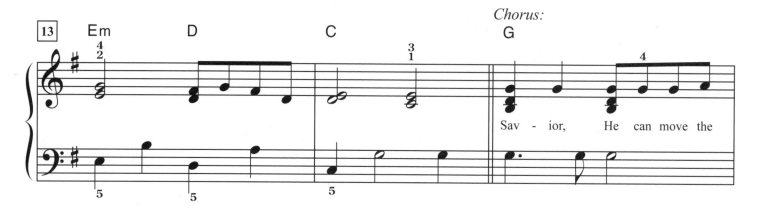

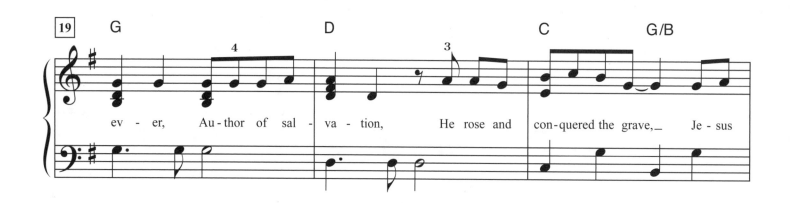

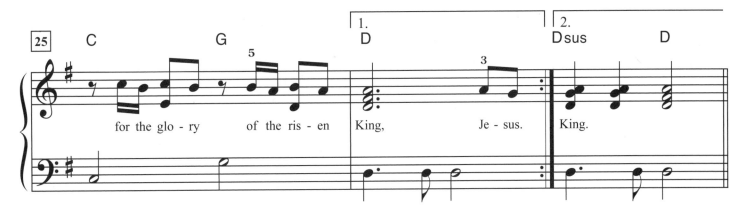

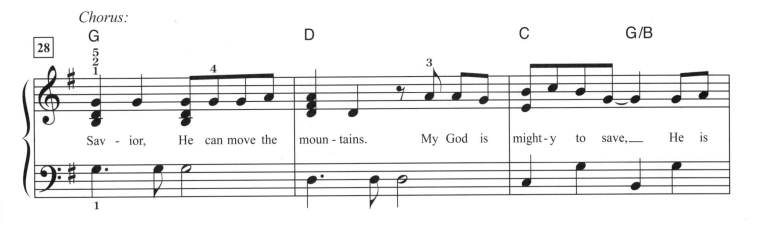

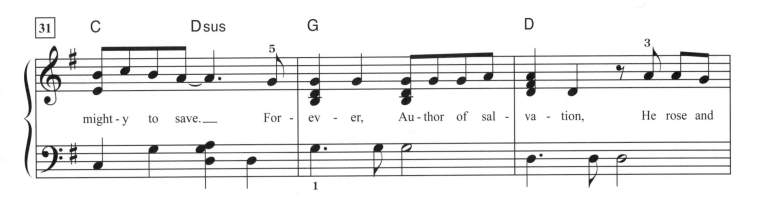

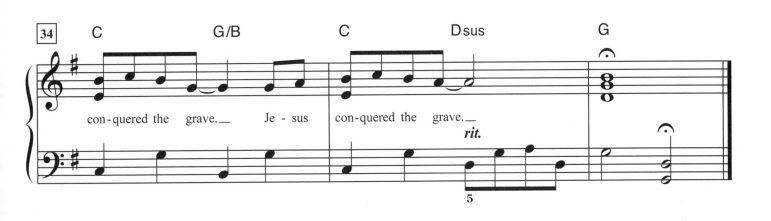

MAJESTY

(Here I Am)

Words and Music by
Martin Smith and Stuart Garrard
Arranged by Carol Tornquist

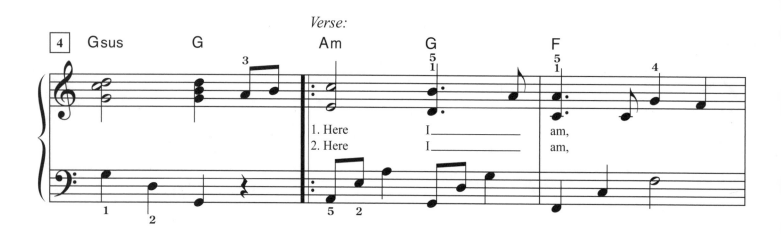

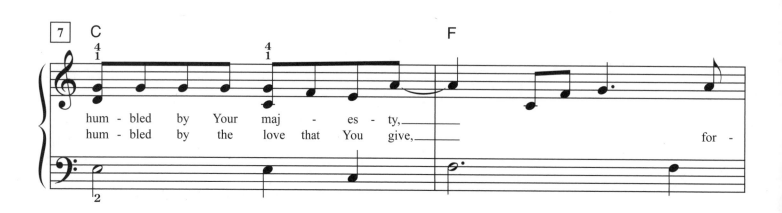

© 2004 CURIOUS? MUSIC UK (PRS)
All Rights in the U.S. and Canada Administered at EMICMGPublishing.com
All Rights Reserved   Used by Permission

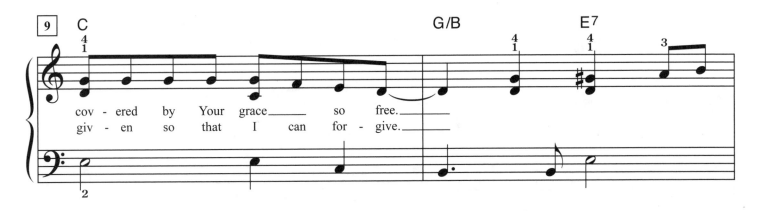

cov - ered by Your grace_____ so free._____
giv - en so that I can for - give._____

Here I_____ am,
Here I_____ stand,

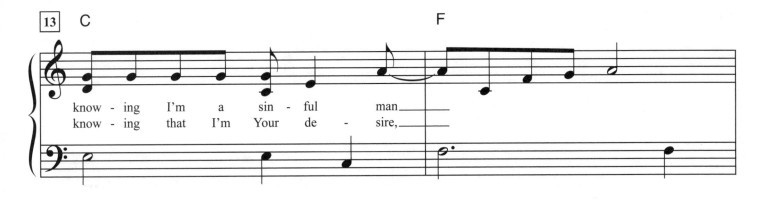

know - ing I'm a sin - ful man_____
know - ing that I'm Your de - sire,_____

cov - ered by the blood of the Lamb._____
sanc - ti - fied by glo - ry and fire._____

Chorus:

Now I've found the great-est love of all is

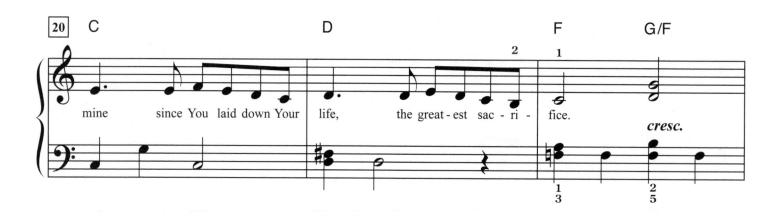

mine since You laid down Your life, the great-est sac-ri-fice.

cresc.

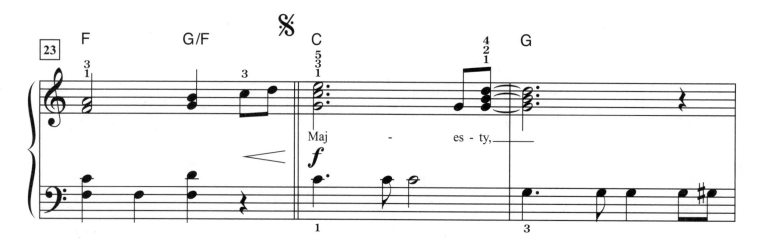

Maj - es - ty,

f

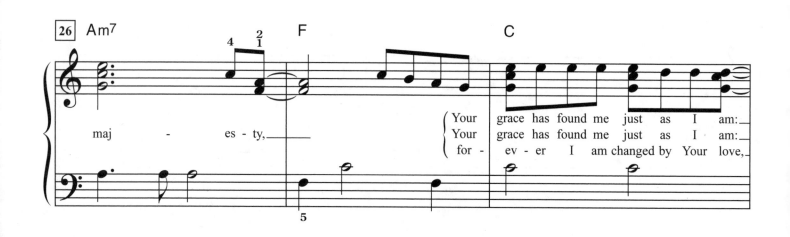

maj - es - ty,

Your grace has found me just as I am:
Your grace has found me just as I am:
for - ev - er I am changed by Your love,

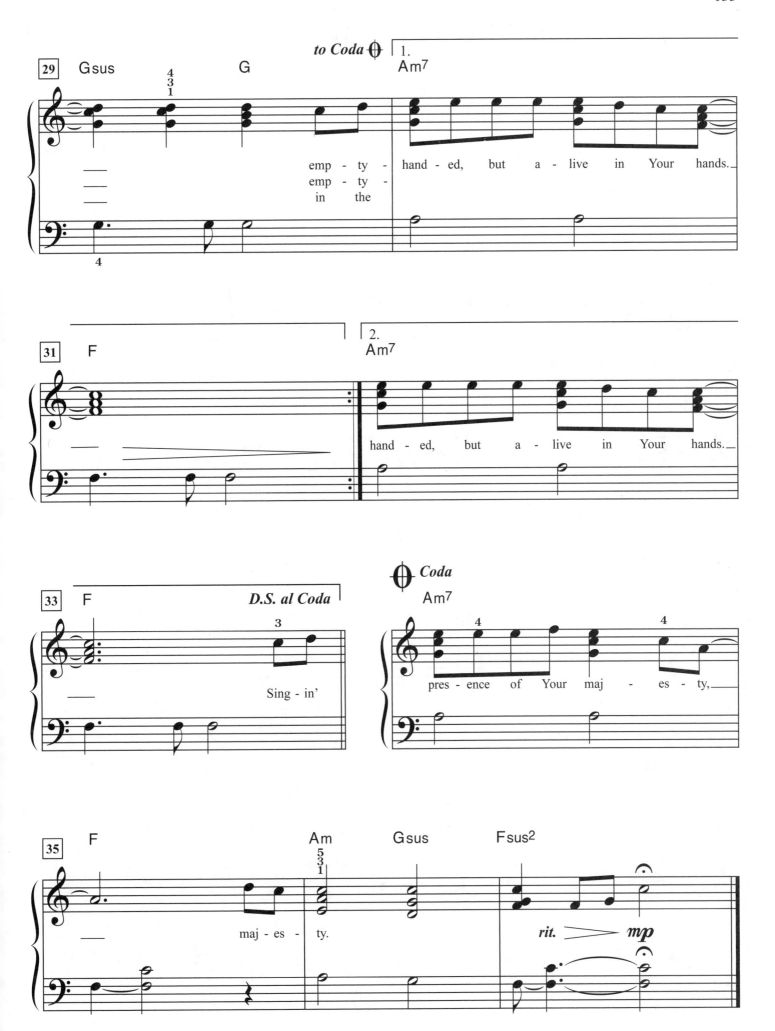

MORE LOVE, MORE POWER

Words and Music by Jude Del Hierro
Arranged by Carol Tornquist

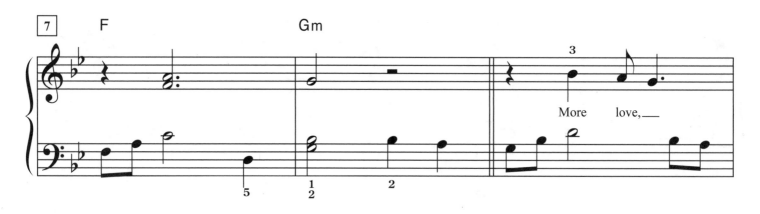

© 1987 MERCY/VINEYARD PUBLISHING (ASCAP)
Administered in North America by MUSIC SERVICES, INC. on behalf of VINEYARD MUSIC USA
All Rights Reserved   Used by Permission

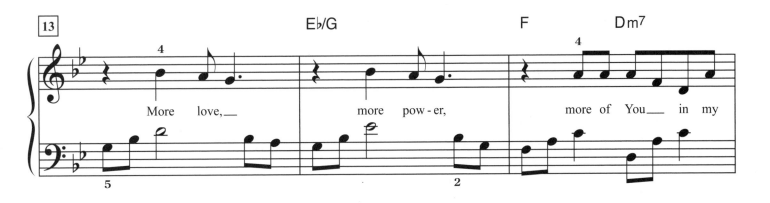

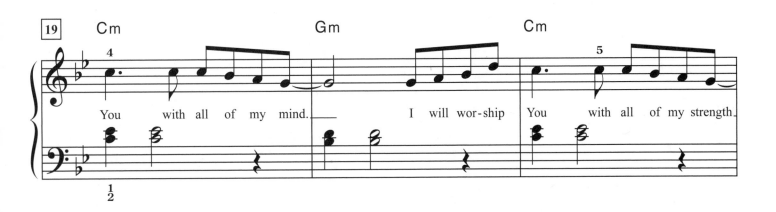

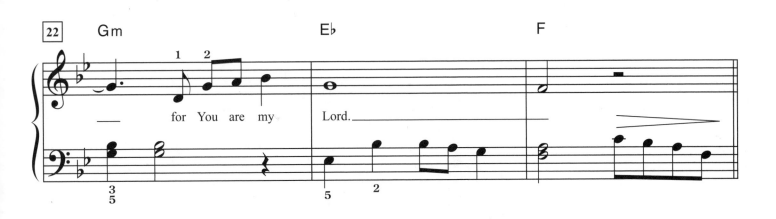

OUR GOD

Words and Music by
Jesse Reeves, Chris Tomlin, Matt Redman and Jonas Myrin
Arranged by Carol Tornquist

© 2010 SHOUT! PUBLISHING (APRA) (Administered in the U.S. and Canada at EMICMGPublishing.com),
THANKYOU MUSIC (PRS) (Administered worldwide at EMICMGPublishing.com excluding Europe which is Administered by kingswaysongs.com),
WORSHIPTOGETHER.COM SONGS, SIXSTEPS MUSIC, VAMOS PUBLISHING and
SAID AND DONE MUSIC (Administered at EMICMGPublishing.com)
All Rights Reserved   Used by Permission

OPEN THE EYES OF MY HEART

Words and Music by Paul Baloche
Arranged by Carol Tornquist

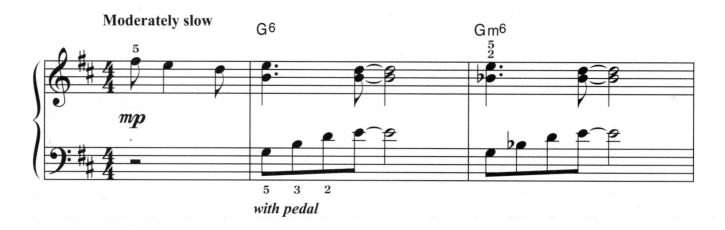

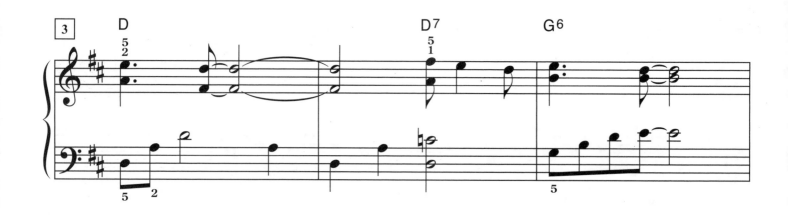

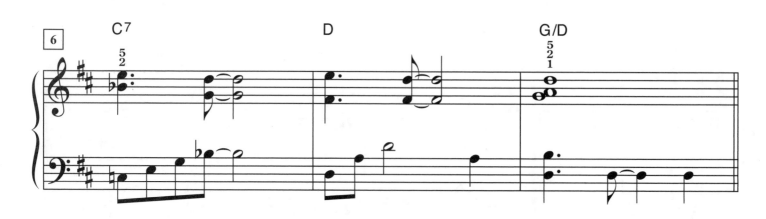

© 1997 INTEGRITY'S HOSANNA! MUSIC
All Rights Administered at EMICMGPublishing.com
All Rights Reserved   Used by Permission

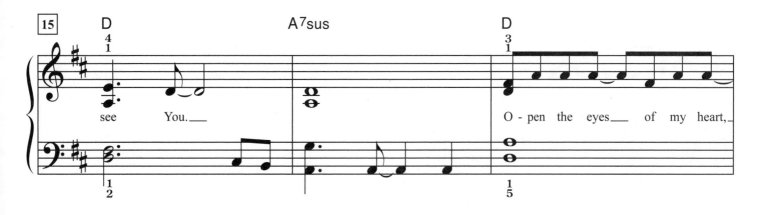

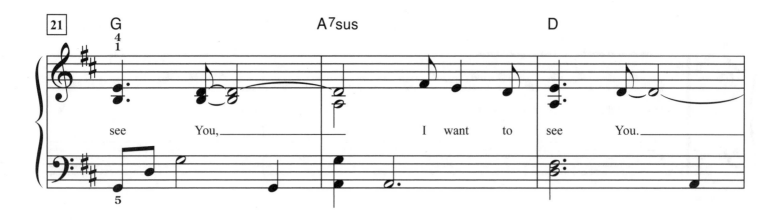

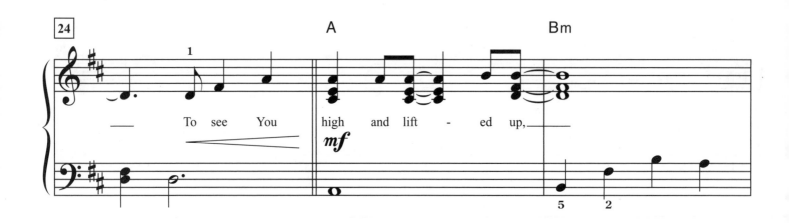

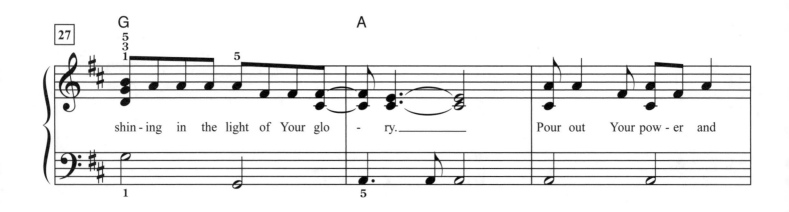

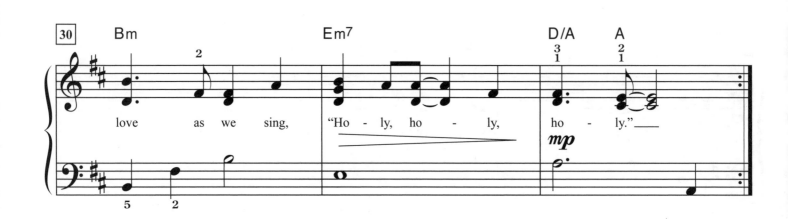

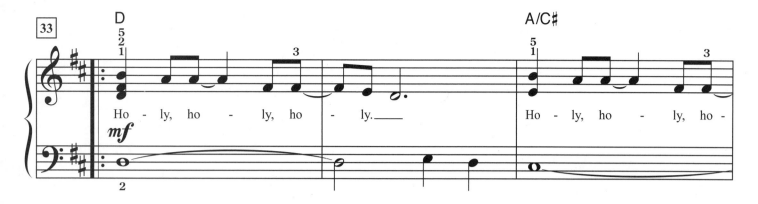

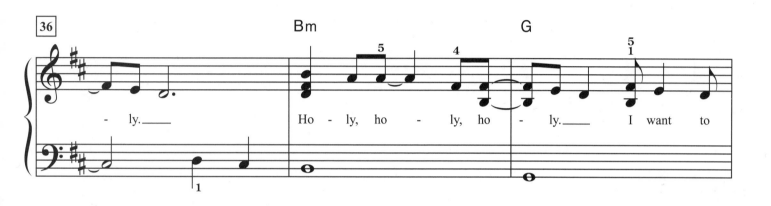

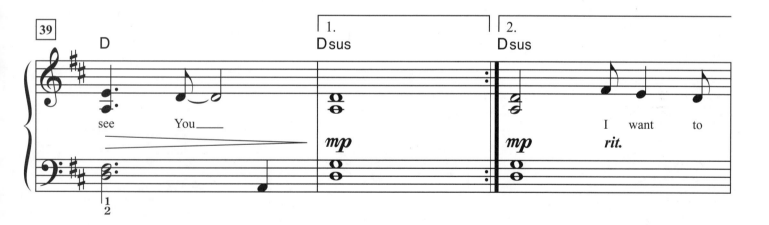

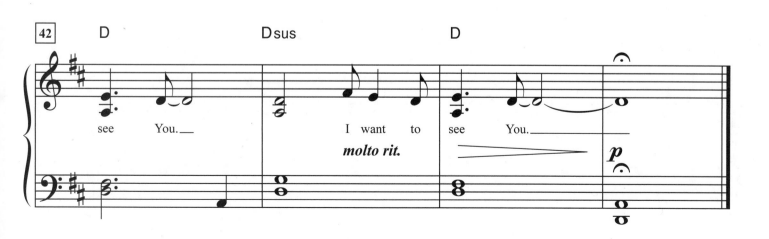

REVELATION SONG

Words and Music by Jennie Lee Riddle
Arranged by Carol Tornquist

© 2004 GATEWAY CREATE PUB. (BMI)
All Rights Administered at EMICMGPublishing.com
All Rights Reserved   Used by Permission

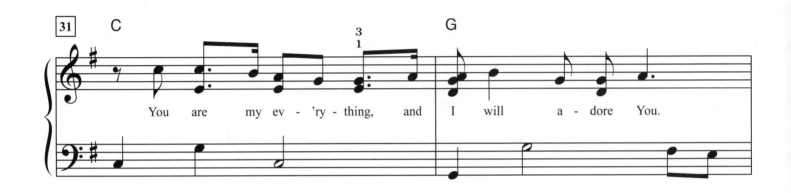

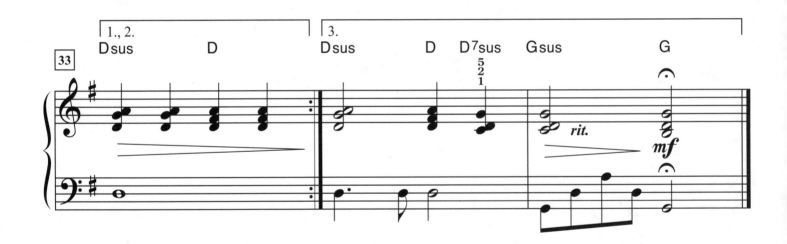

Verse 2:
Clothed in rainbows of living color,
Flashes of lightning, rolls of thunder,
Blessing and honor, strength and glory and power
Be to You, the only wise King.
(To Chorus:)

Verse 3:
Filled with wonder, awestruck wonder,
At the mention of Your name.
Jesus, Your name is power, breath, and living water,
Such a marvelous mystery.
(To Chorus:)

SHOUT TO THE LORD

Words and Music by Darlene Zschech
Arranged by Carol Tornquist

© 1993 HILLSONG PUBLISHING (APRA)
All Rights in the U.S. and Canada Administered at EMICMGPublishing.com
All Rights Reserved   Used by Permission

name.____ I sing for joy___ at the work___ of Your hands.__ For -

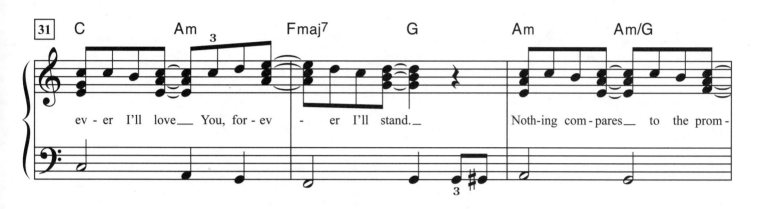

ev - er I'll love__ You, for - ev - er I'll stand.__ Noth-ing com-pares__ to the prom -

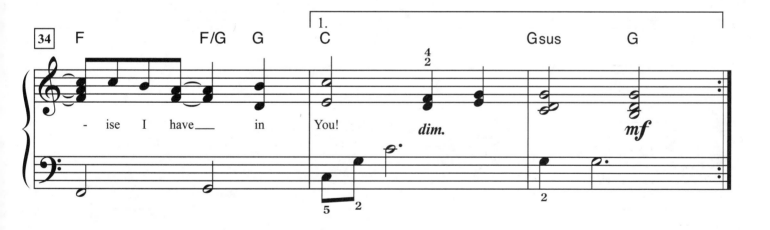

1.

- ise I have__ in You! *dim.* *mf*

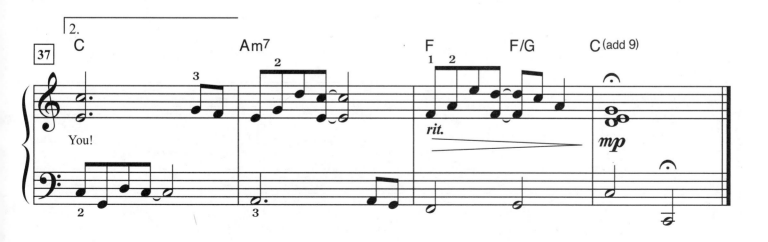

2.

You! *rit.* *mp*

SING TO THE KING

Words and Music by Billy Foote
Arranged by Carol Tornquist

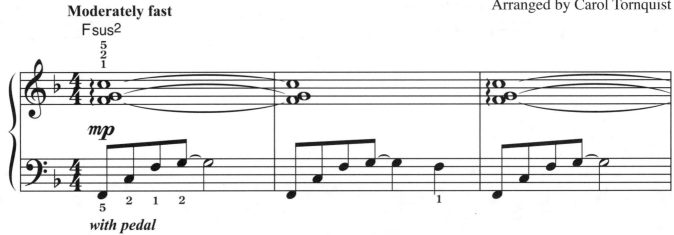

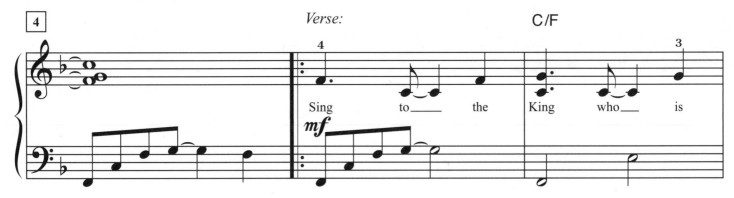

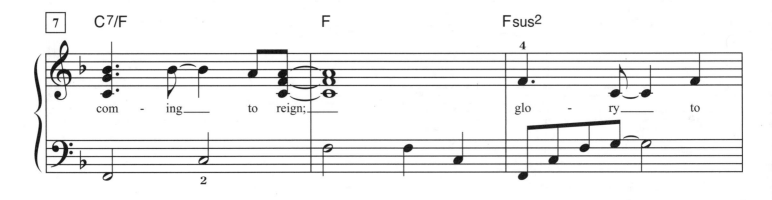

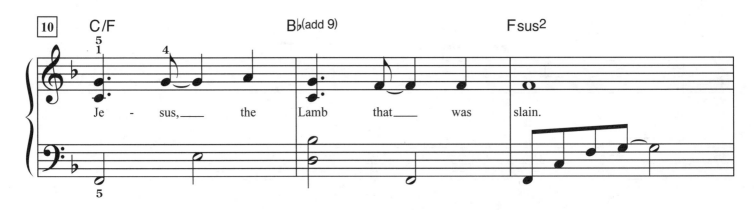

© 2003 WORSHIPTOGETHER.COM SONGS and SIXSTEPS MUSIC
All Rights Administered at EMICMGPublishing.com
All Rights Reserved   Used by Permission

UNTITLED HYMN

(Come to Jesus)

Words and Music by Chris Rice
Arranged by Carol Tornquist

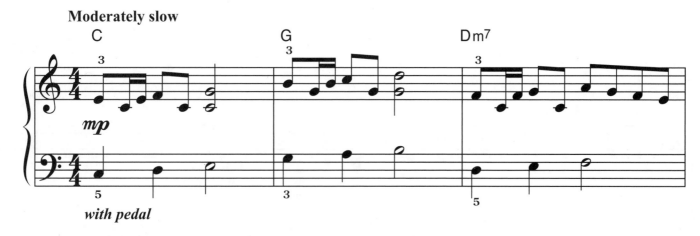

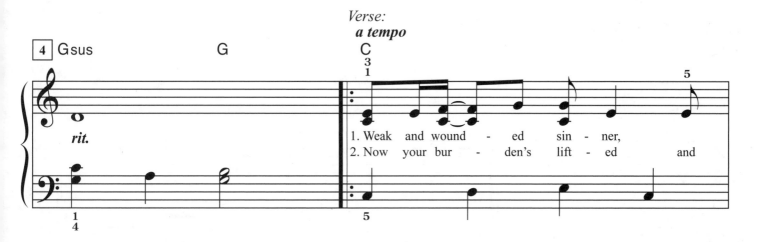

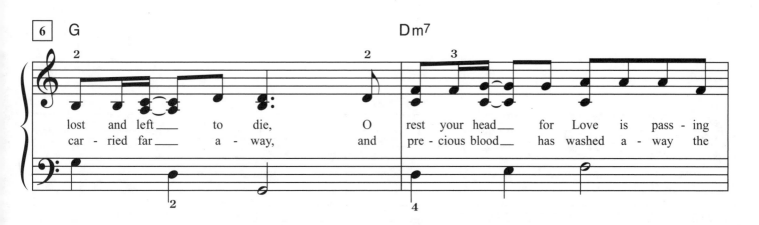

© 2003 CLUMSY FLY MUSIC
All Rights Administered by WORD MUSIC, LLC
All Rights Reserved   Used by Permission

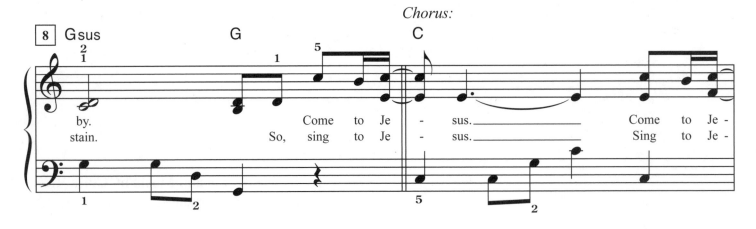

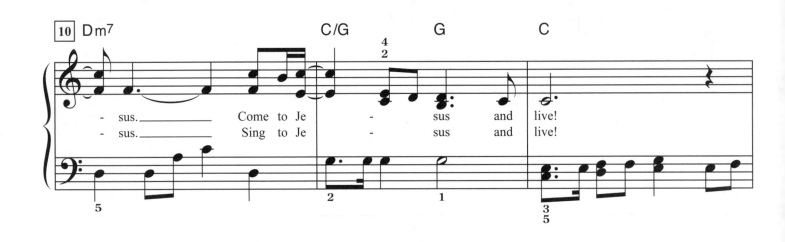

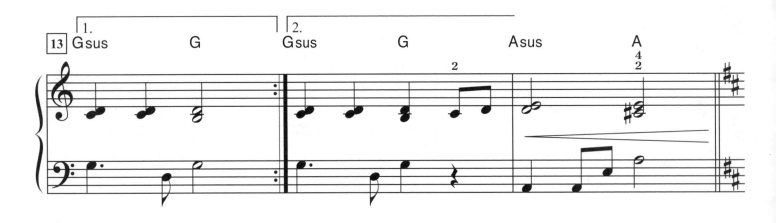

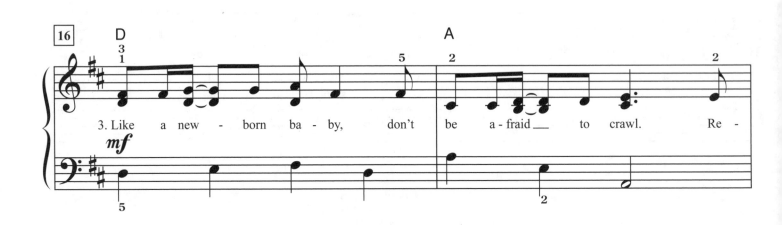

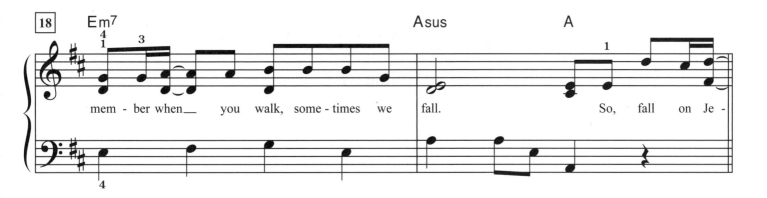

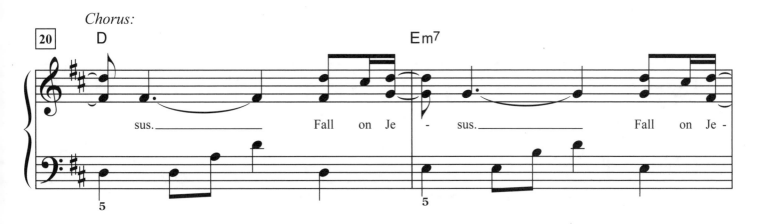

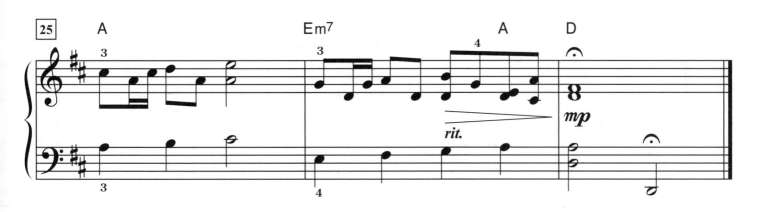

TAKE MY LIFE

(Holiness)

Words and Music by Scott Underwood
Arranged by Carol Tornquist

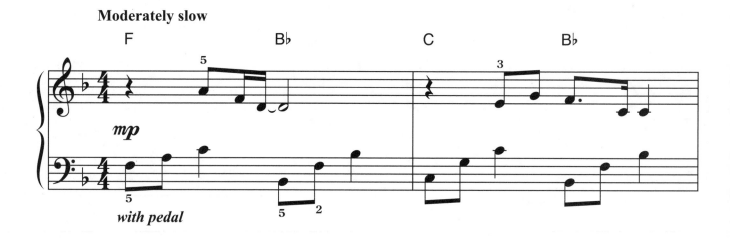

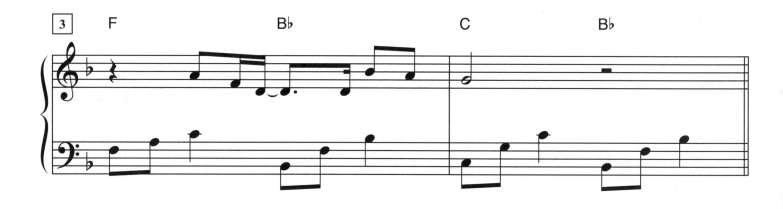

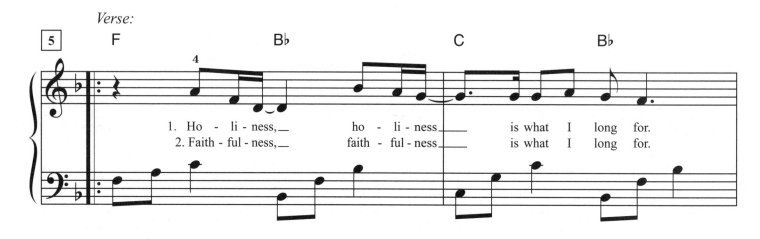

1. Ho - li - ness,___ ho - li - ness___ is what I long for.
2. Faith - ful - ness,___ faith - ful - ness___ is what I long for.

© 1994 MERCY/VINEYARD PUBLISHING (ASCAP)
Administered in North America by MUSIC SERVICES, INC. on behalf of VINEYARD MUSIC USA
All Rights Reserved   Used by Permission

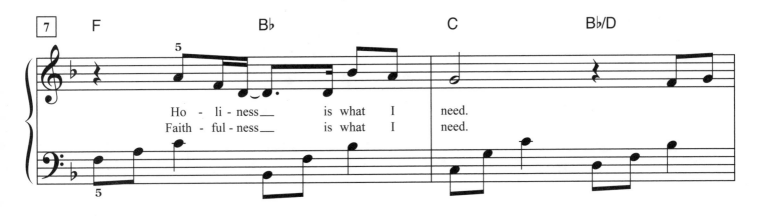

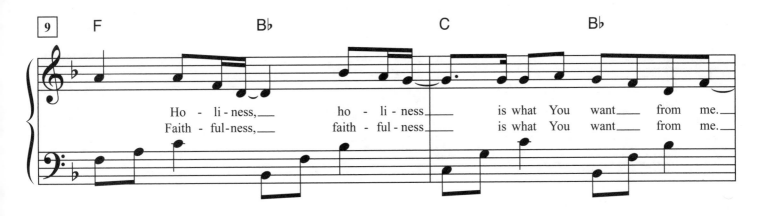

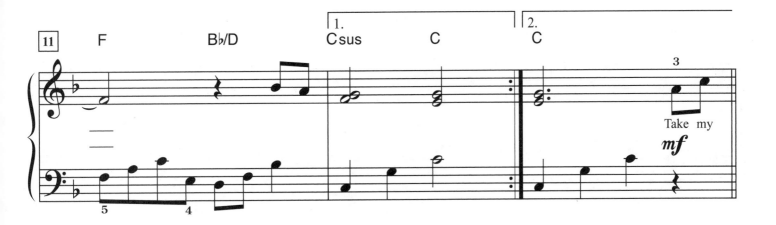

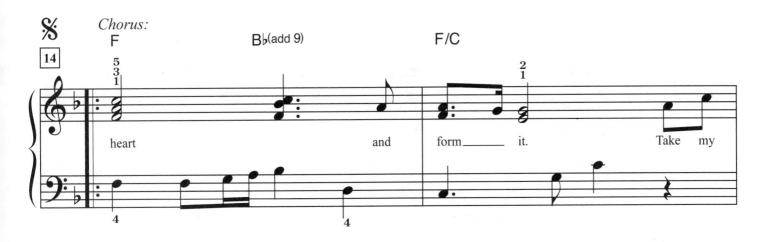

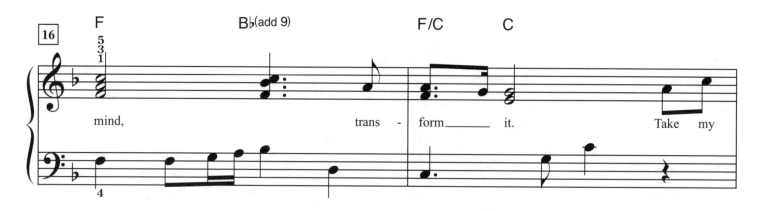

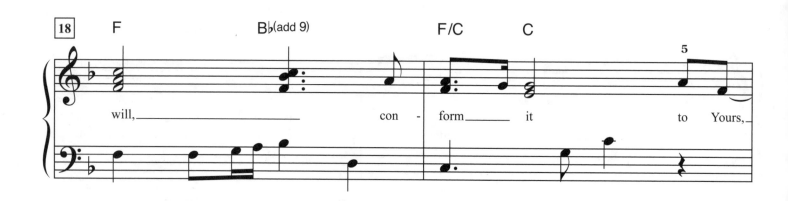

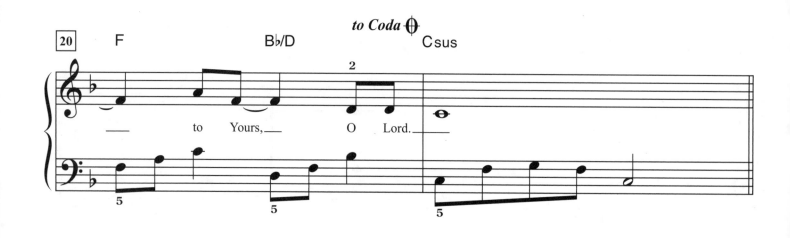

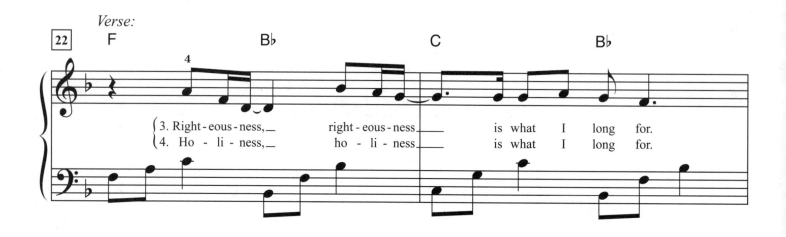

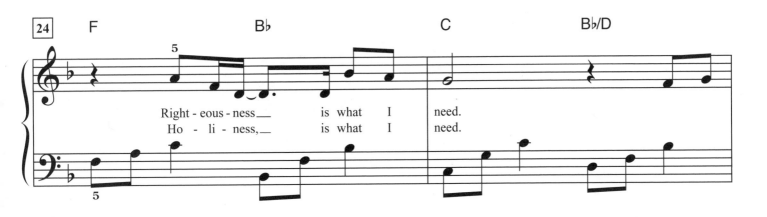

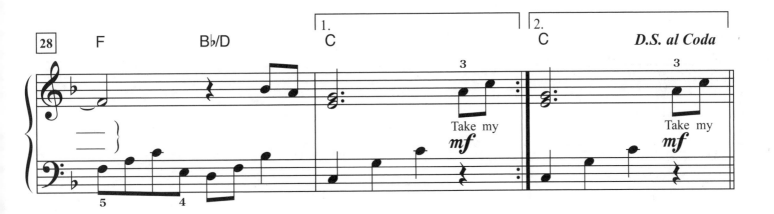

WE FALL DOWN

Words and Music by Chris Tomlin
Arranged by Carol Tornquist

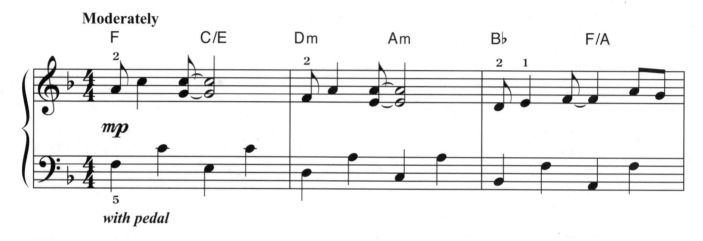

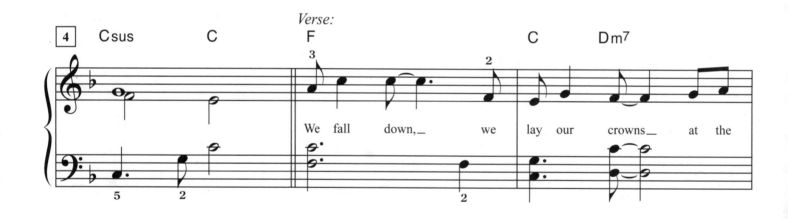

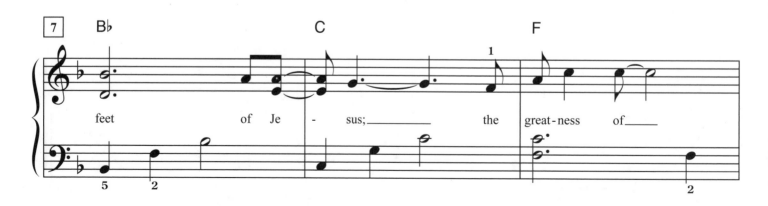

© 1998 WORSHIPTOGETHER.COM SONGS
All Rights Administered at EMICMGPublishing.com
All Rights Reserved   Used by Permission

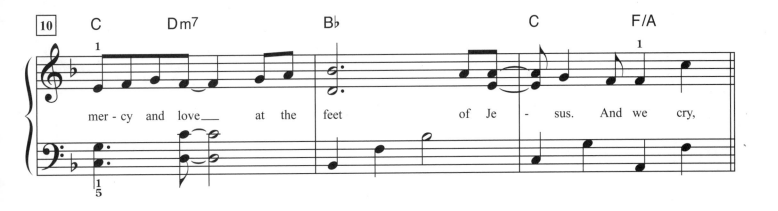

mer - cy and love___ at the feet of Je - sus. And we cry,

Chorus:

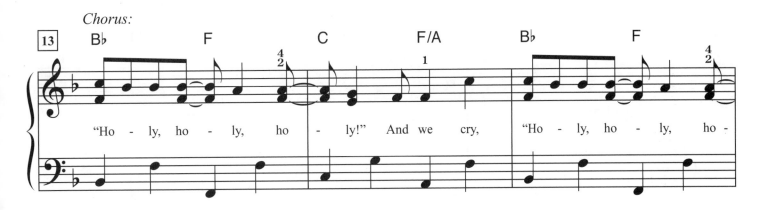

"Ho - ly, ho - ly, ho - ly!" And we cry, "Ho - ly, ho - ly, ho -

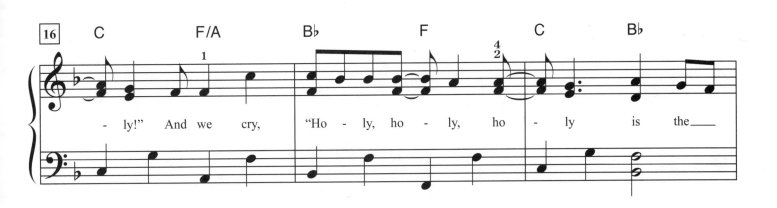

- ly!" And we cry, "Ho - ly, ho - ly, ho - ly is the___

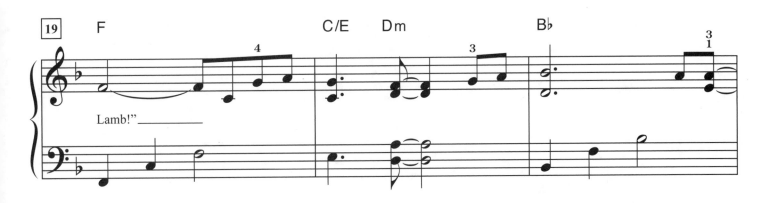

Lamb!"___

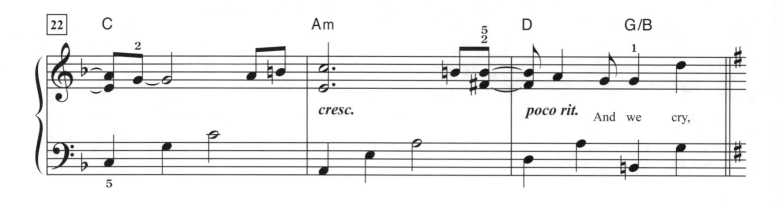

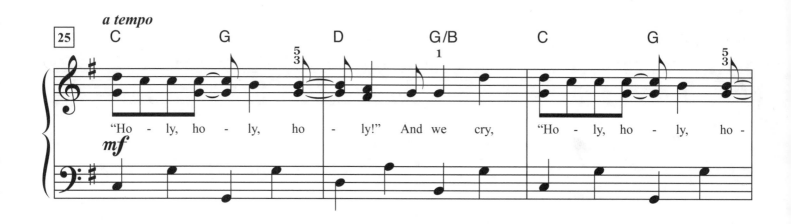

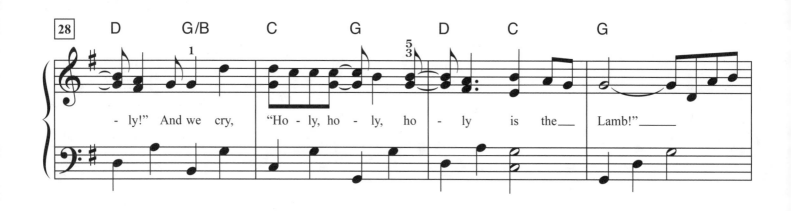

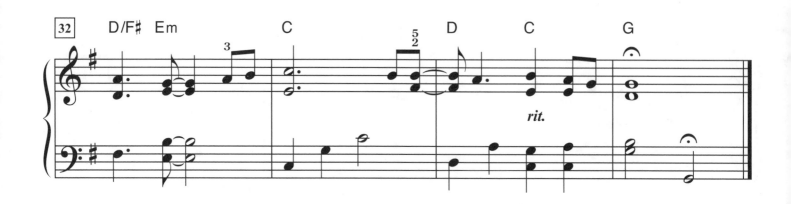

THE WONDERFUL CROSS

Words and Music by
Chris Tomlin, J.D. Walt and Jesse Reeves
Arranged by Carol Tornquist

© 2000 WORSHIPTOGETHER.COM SONGS and SIXSTEPS MUSIC
All Rights Administered at EMICMGPublishing.com
All Rights Reserved   Used by Permission

Chorus:

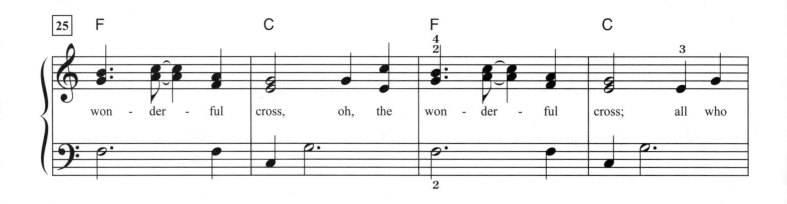

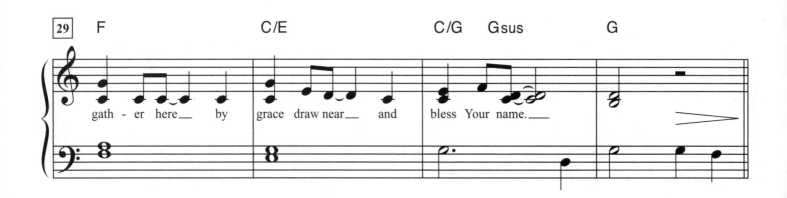

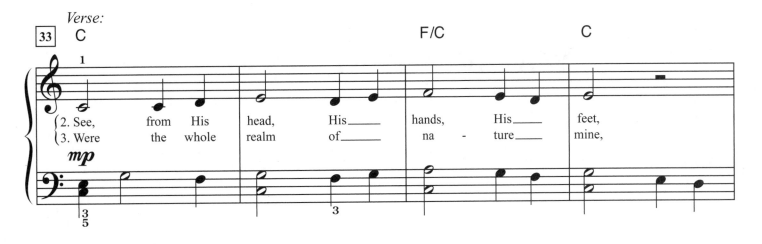

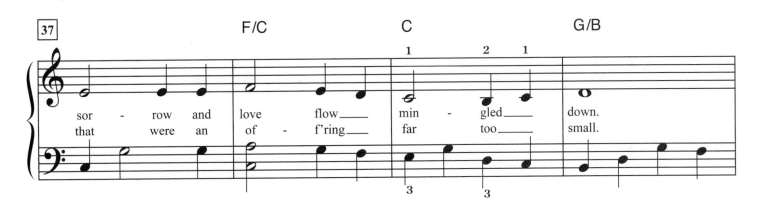

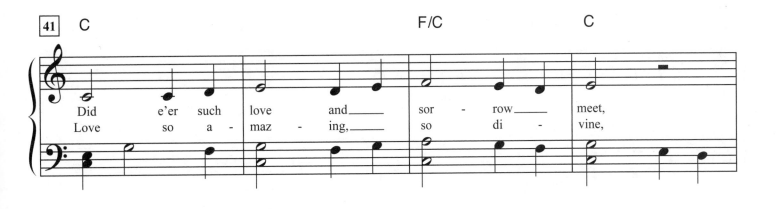

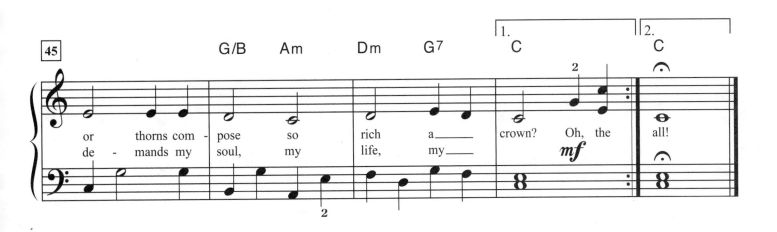

YOU ARE MY ALL IN ALL

Words and Music by Dennis L. Jernigan
Arranged by Carol Tornquist

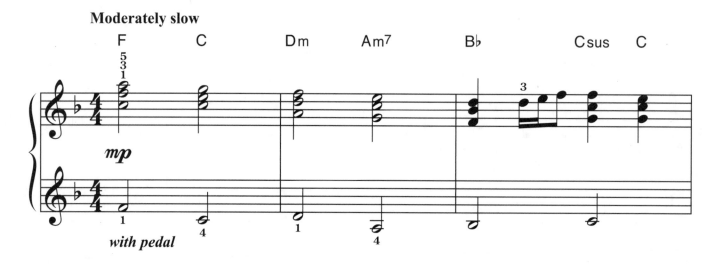

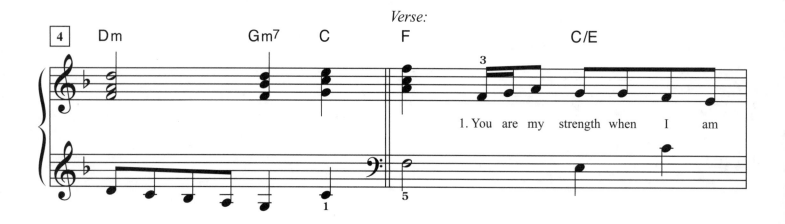

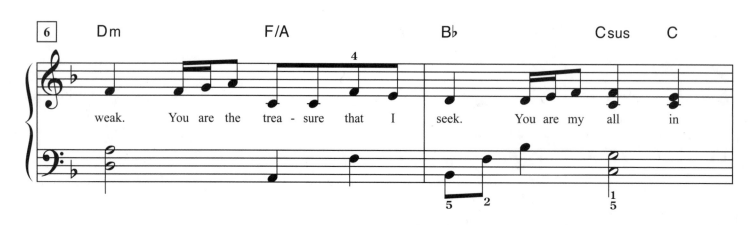

© 1991 SHEPHERD'S HEART MUSIC, INC.
All Rights Administered by PRAISECHARTS
All Rights Reserved   Used by Permission

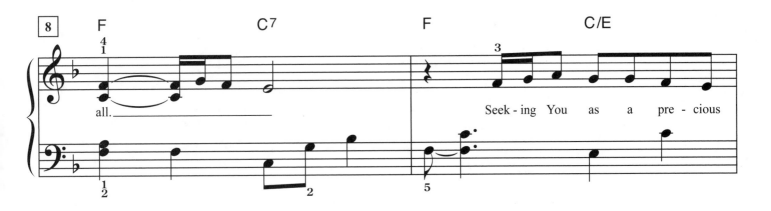

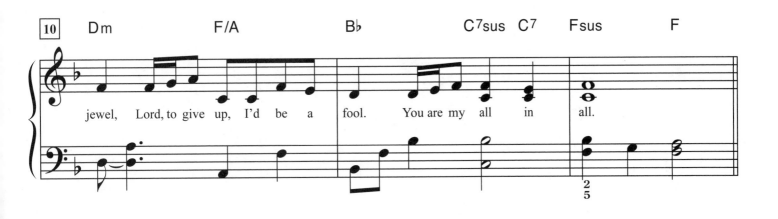

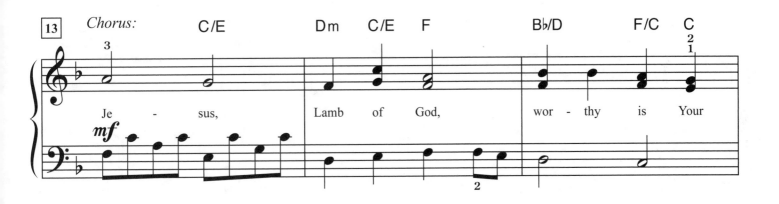

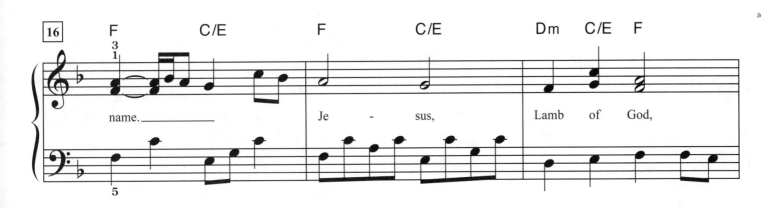

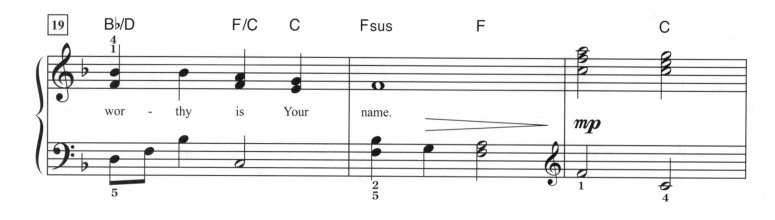

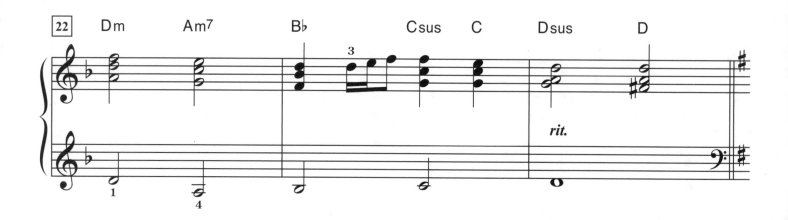

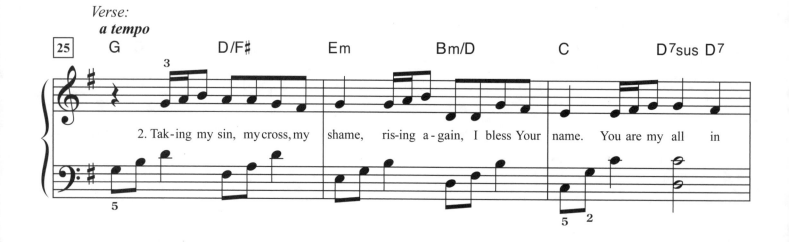

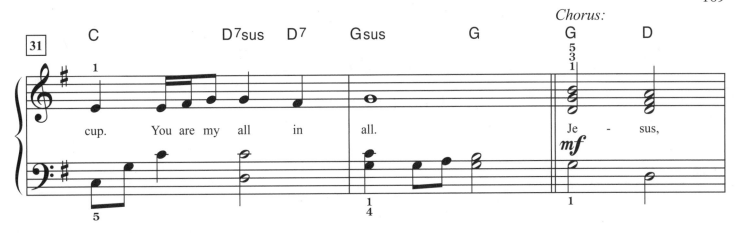

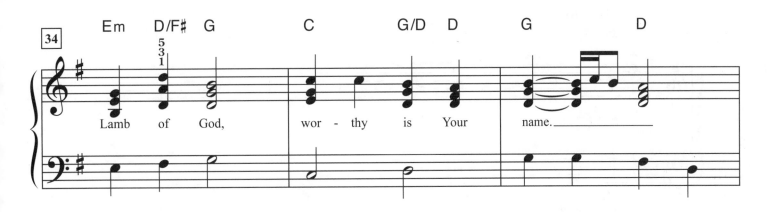

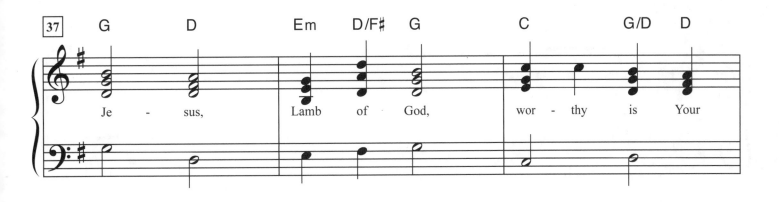

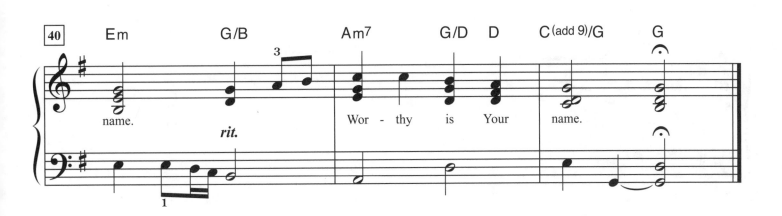

YOU ARE MY KING

(Amazing Love)

Words and Music by
Billy James Foote
Arranged by Carol Tornquist

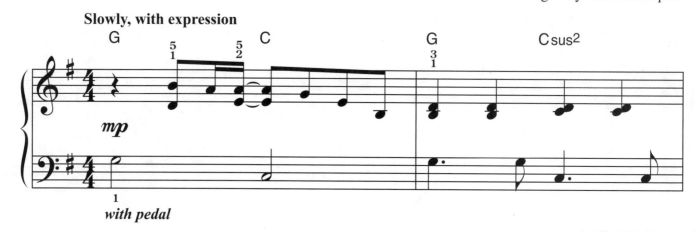

Verse:

I'm for-giv-en be - cause You were___ for-sak-en.

© 1999 WORSHIPTOGETHER.COM SONGS
All Rights Administered at EMICMGPublishing.com
All Rights Reserved   Used by Permission

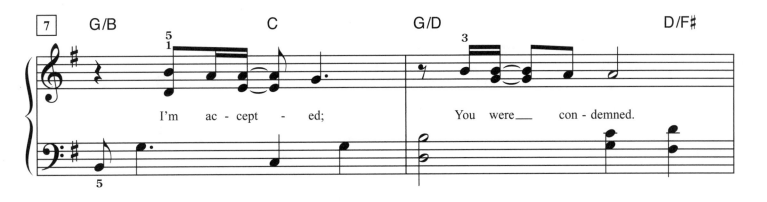

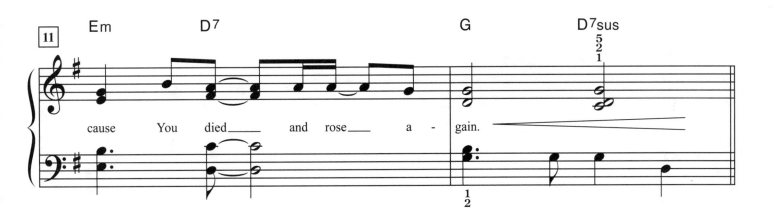

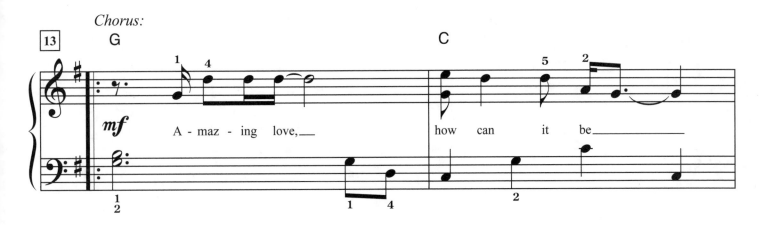

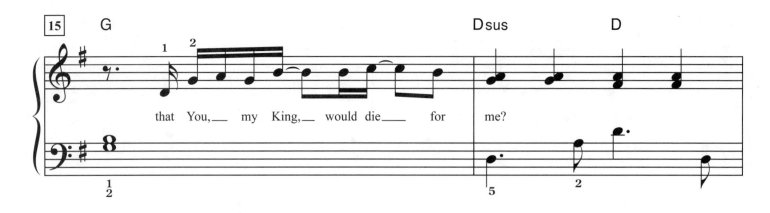

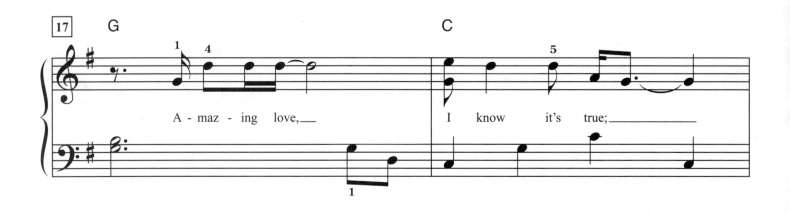

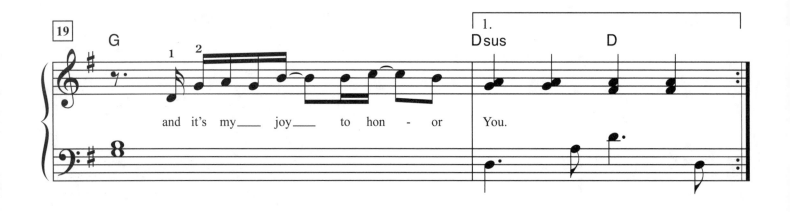

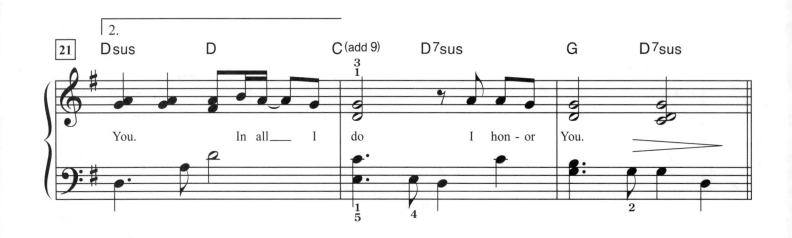

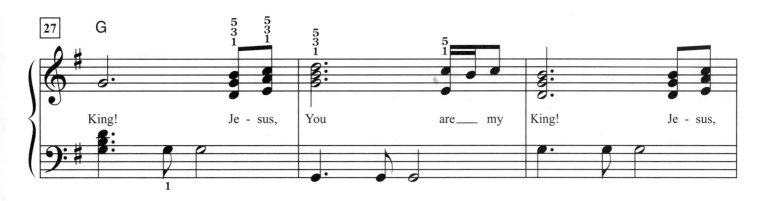

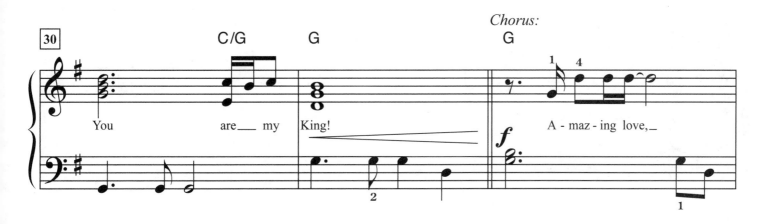

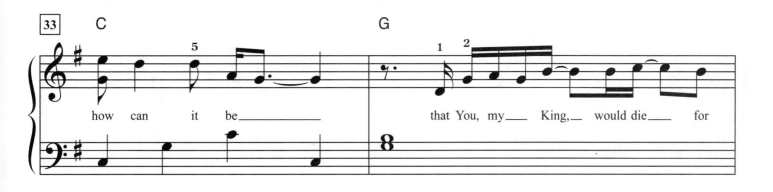

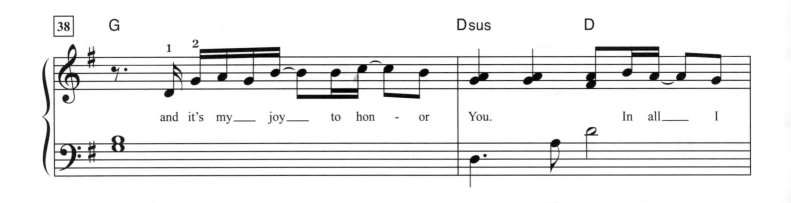

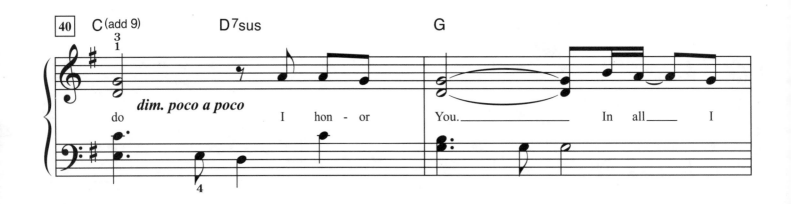

YOUR GRACE IS ENOUGH

Words and Music by Matt Maher
Arranged by Carol Tornquist

© 2004 THANKYOU MUSIC (PRS) and SPIRITANDSONG.COM PUBLISHING
All Rights for THANKYOU MUSIC (PRS) (Administered worldwide at EMICMGPublishing.com
excluding Europe which is administered by kingswaysongs.com)
All Rights Reserved   Used by Permission

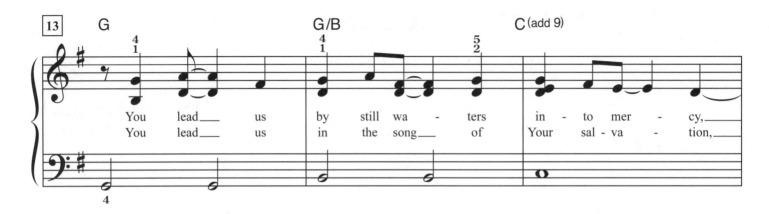

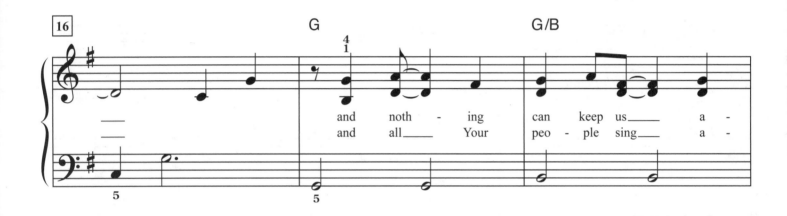

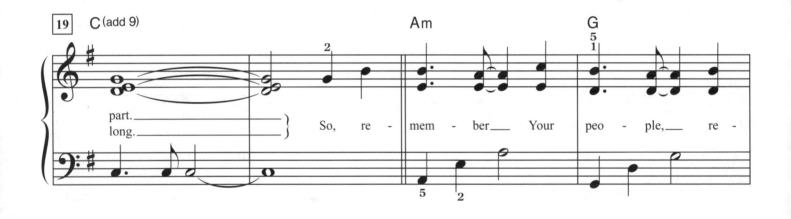

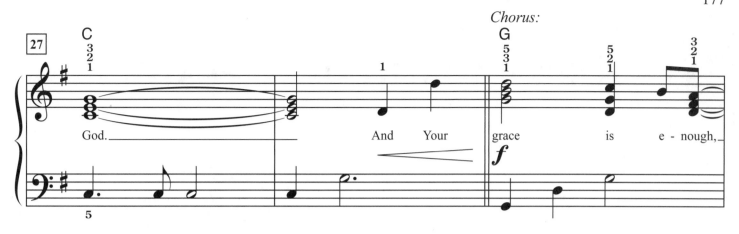

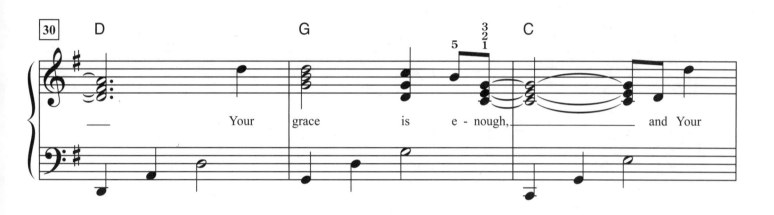

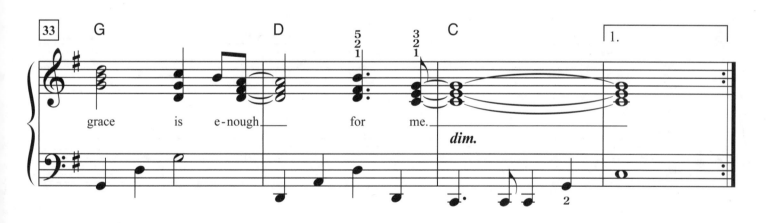

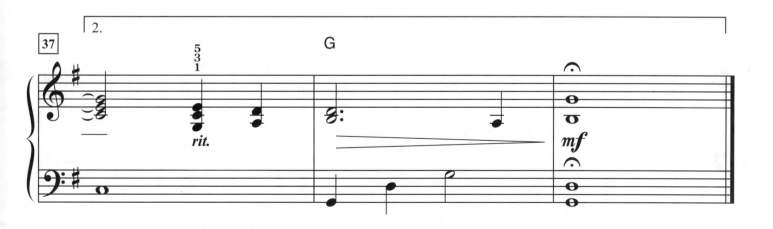

YOU'RE WORTHY OF MY PRAISE

Words and Music by David Ruis
Arranged by Carol Tornquist

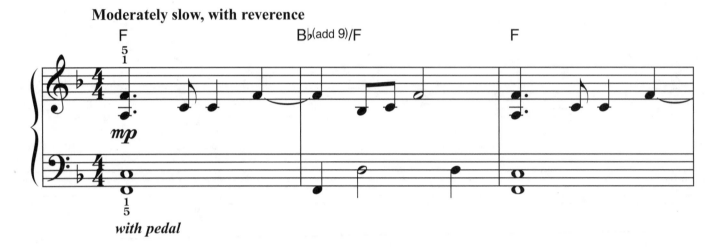

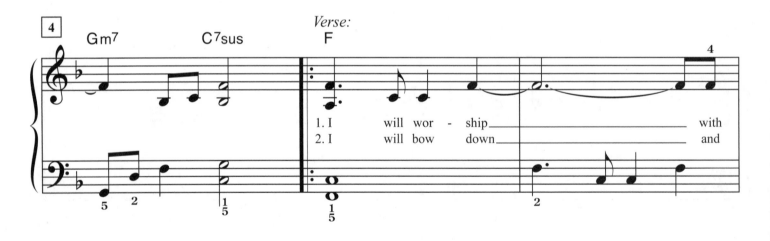

© 1991 SHADE TREE MUSIC and MARANATHA! PRAISE, INC.
All Rights Administered by MUSIC SERVICES, INC.
All Rights Reserved   Used by Permission

with all of my strength.
give You ev - 'ry - thing.

I will seek You_____ all of my days.
I will lift up_____ my eyes to Your throne.

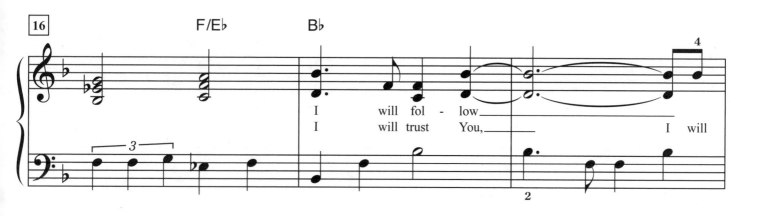

I will fol - low_____
I will trust You,_____ I will

Chorus:

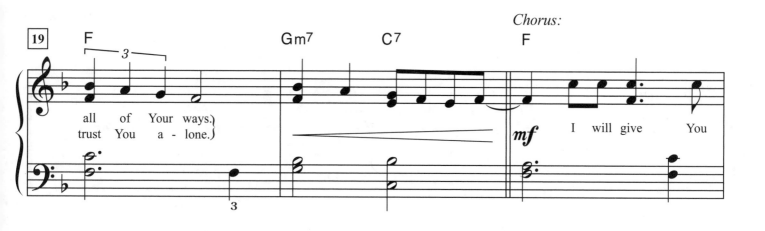

all of Your ways.)
trust You a - lone.)

mf I will give You

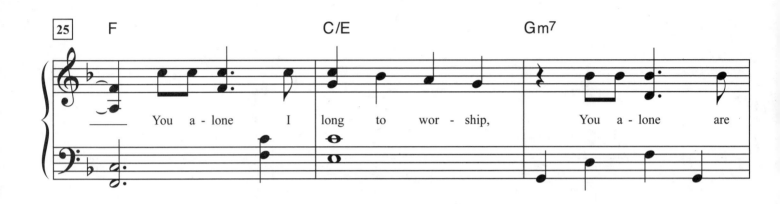

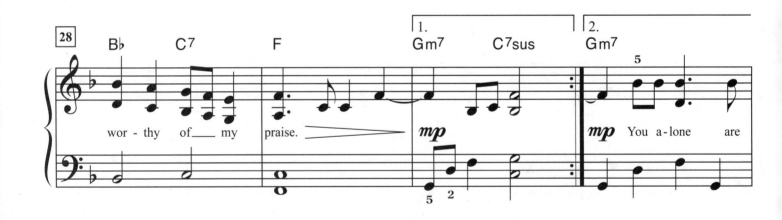

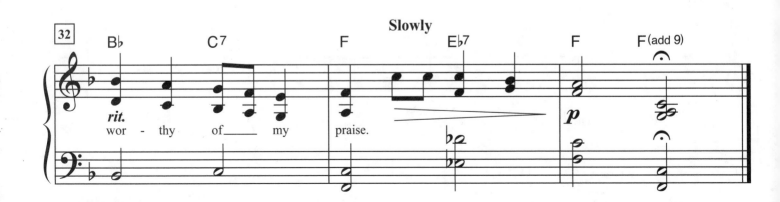